THE WORLD IN 1900 *a colour portrait*

MARC WALTER AND SABINE ARQUÉ
PREFACE BY JEAN-CHRISTOPHE RUFIN

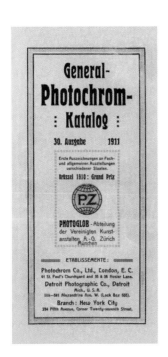

The images in this book were all taken from a catalogue produced by Photoglob Zurich in 1911 (above).

Half-title page: Climbers on an ice ridge in the Alps
Title page: Quai des Alpes, Zurich

Authors' acknowledgments
The authors wish to express their gratitude to Mr Gion Schneller, Director of Photoglob AG, who has kindly permitted them to gather the information necessary for the publication of this book. Thanks are also due to Blandine Gallix for her advice, and to Emile Boismoreau, Florence Cailly, Emmanuel Ducamp, Emilie Greenberg and Philippe Marchand for their help with documentation and for their friendly support.

Translated from the French *Portrait d'un monde en couleurs* by Philip Watson

First published in the United Kingdom in 2007 by
Thames & Hudson Ltd, 181A High Holborn, London WC1V 7QX

www.thamesandhudson.com

Original edition ©2006 by Editions Solar, an imprint of Place des Editeurs, Paris
This edition © 2007 Thames & Hudson Ltd, London

British Library Cataloguing-in-Publication Data
A catalogue record for this book is available from the British Library

ISBN: 978-0-500-28705-7

Printed and bound in China

Contents

Preface

Here is the elsewhere we have been dreaming of: an elsewhere of distant places long thought to be familiar that have suddenly taken on a new life.

Today's travellers suffer endlessly from having been beaten to their destinations. Seen Venice? Of course you have. But how does it feel to see it alone and for the first time? What is it like when you can still feel the barely departed shadow of Casanova, or pass Ruskin or Wagner in the street? With luck, you could experience that sensation on certain winter evenings in the side streets of the Dorsoduro. But who could hope to do so on the Grand Canal, in broad daylight, between the Salute and the Daniele Hotel?

This is precisely the magic of these photochrome plates. Their unexpected use of colour makes them strangely fascinating and draws us in. By some remarkable, unique effect that ordinary photographic plates never achieve, we find ourselves totally arborbed in this long-vanished world, and we feel the interval of time all the more powerfully. We recognize the monuments, but their solitary scale, their frequent silence, the horse-drawn cabs, the children in their smocks and the well-dressed women – they prove to us that we really are elsewhere.

The feeling of disorientation is even stronger in the 'exotic' views. Algiers, Cairo and India are restored to us through details that may well have disappeared today, but that survive in our subconscious like a sort of improbable, dreamed-up Orient – the imagined East of Delacroix, Flaubert and Lear. The world of photochromes is poetic in a way that no contemporary spectacle ever could be, giving rise to nostalgia without a hint of sorrow, and allowing us glimpses of those rare moments in which the eternal human condition is revealed.

Jean-Christophe Rufin

(opposite) The Doge's Palace and Piazzetta, Venice
(above) The port of Algiers and the Admiralty building

Travels in colour

The nineteenth century: incredible, abundant, fascinating . . . Railways, the telephone, electricity, the motor car, cinema, photography: all of these inventions – to name but a few – surfaced between 1830 and 1890. By the century's end a new era was truly dawning. Consider the progress that this technical revolution brought for travellers: in 1890 the Orient Express could reach Constantinople in six days, when the same journey ninety years earlier could take almost two months, and in somewhat different conditions. In 1869, the year the Suez Canal opened, Edmond About travelled to Egypt. He took the train from Paris; within sixteen hours he had arrived in Marseilles; and six days later he disembarked at Alexandria. Sixty years earlier, Chateaubriand had spent a month and a half just getting from Alexandria to Tunis . . . and having hurried to Alexandria after cutting short his visit to Cairo, he had to wait days for a favourable wind. A similar story applied to crossing the Atlantic, from Le Havre to New York: it took four or five days in the last years of the nineteenth century, as against a fortnight in 1840 – and that was with good sea conditions. As for travelling across the American continent, in 1884 About described 'these moving colonies that the New York train brings to San Francisco in five and a half days, across 5,350 kilometres, suffering neither from hunger nor from thirst, nor even from pins and needles' – nothing like the slow and dangerous journey made by the pioneers forty years before, who would take months to reach the West.

Some of the progress made over half a century can be measured through these examples. And if we think sixteen hours is an eternity for travelling between Paris and Marseille, we have had to wait another 150 years for the most advanced technology – high-speed trains – to cut the time by three quarters. It is a small advance compared to the feats achieved in the last fifty years of the nineteenth century.

The time of travelling photographers

Travellers at the end of the nineteenth century thus had modern means of transport at their disposal, and they were able to take advantage of them to discover the world. Talk was no longer of expeditions, but of scientific or photographic 'missions', or 'cruises' (like the later Citroën Croisère Noire in 1924–25, a sponsored motor journey to Africa). Here were the beginnings of the sort of tourism we might recognize today. In fact, from 1880 onwards everything was in place for the rise of leisure travel. The East (Near and Far), Africa and South-east Asia were in the throes of colonization; the Americans had put Native peoples into 'reservations'; the English were in India, Cambodia, China and Malaysia; the French were in Indochina, North Africa, sub-Saharan Africa . . . In sum, the planet had become safe, 'white', and one no longer needed to be an adventurer at heart to go there.

(preceding pages) A woman from Bethlehem. Left: Print from an original negative by Félix Bonfils, *c.* 1870. Right: Photochrome taken from Bonfils' negative, *c.* 1890

(opposite) Hôtel de la Poste,
Simplon Pass, *c.* 1890
(left) Bowder Stone in the Lake
District
(right) Bootblacks in Cairo

Pioneers had opened the way, building the roads, bridges and tunnels, laying railways and constructing hotels. And there was something else to reckon with: photography, which took a decisive step forward with the appearance of the Kodak camera. 'Press the button, we do the rest', proclaimed the slogan of the American company Eastman, which in 1888 put this invention within everyone's reach, and first and foremost into the hands of the new tourists.

In the fifty or sixty years since the invention of photography, and since the 1850s and 1860s in particular, the new technique had evolved so far that practically all the great sites, monuments and classic places of interest on the planet had been photographed. Photographer-travellers journeyed all over the world with their equipment, loading up mules or camels with their glass plates, chemicals and all the precious requisites of the dark room. Between 1849 and 1852 Maxime Du Camp and Gustave Flaubert went to Egypt; at the same time the German Wilhelm Hammerschmidt, who kept a shop in Cairo, travelled the Valley of the Nile up to Abu Simbel. Gustave Le Gray, photographer to the court of Napoleon III, headed for Cairo in 1860. Henri Béchard, who arrived in Egypt shortly before the opening of the Suez Canal and who also made for Cairo, was to join forces with another photographer, Jean-Pascal Sebah. In 1867, Félix Bonfils and his wife Lydie moved to Beirut. Between 1857 and 1860, the Englishman Francis Frith crossed Egypt, Palestine and Syria. In 1862

his compatriot Francis Bedford accompanied the future king Edward VII on his Grand Tour. Another Englishman, John Thomson, arrived in Singapore in 1863 before setting off through Thailand, Cambodia, China and Indochina. In 1858, the Italians Felice Beato and his brother Antonio went to Calcutta; Antonio then left for Cairo while Felice went to China and Japan, where he opened the country's first studio, in Yokohama. Another Italian, Carlo Naya, set up a studio in Constantinople before returning to Venice in 1856, where he established his premises on St Mark's Square. During the last three decades of the nineteenth century, other photographers emigrated to Cairo, Port Said, Luxor, Jerusalem, Constantinople, Beirut, Athens, Algiers, Tunis, Calcutta, Bombay, Delhi, Singapore, Hong Kong, and so on. This list of names and places – although far from exhaustive – gives an idea of the position held by photography during the last half of the nineteenth century.

Progress and modernity have their downsides: dehumanization, pollution, and the loss of Nature's pristine purity. Travel accounts from the end of the nineteenth century bear witness to these changes: the world was no longer what it had been. At the hands of entrepreneurs, engineers and industry, Western cities became uninhabitable; cities in the colonies lost their charm and particular character; and, conquered by tourists, 'exotic' countries were changed entirely. 'What is that, and where have we fallen?' complained Pierre Loti in Cairo in 1907.

'You would think that this were Nice, the Riviera or Interlaken, any one of those carnivalesque cities where the bad taste of the whole world has come to frolic during the so-called elegant seasons. . . . Everywhere there is blinding electricity; monstrous hotels, flaunting false luxury with their alluring facades. . . . Countless cabarets overflowing with bottles: all our alcohol, all our Western poisons, poured zealously over Egypt.'

Archives of the planet

Even during this period fears were expressed and people spoke of 'the end of the world'. The speeding up of lifestyles led to a feeling of insecurity, which in turn prompted the creation of numerous associations, societies, archives and missions of every kind in the field of photography.

'In this century of steam and electricity, everything is changing, becoming transformed, even places. Before progress finally completes its destructive work, before this present that is soon to be the past has disappeared forever, we wish to fix it in time, so to speak, in a series of views that we offer to our readers in this album.' This preface – to a project devoted to Syria, Lebanon and Palestine – was drafted by Adrien Bonfils, the son of Félix Bonfils, who took over his father's studio in Beirut in 1885. Moved by a similar feeling, the *British Journal of Photography* proposed setting up global photographic archives. In 1897 the National

Photographic Record Association was founded with the purpose of collecting documents relating to traditional ceremonies and festivals around the world. In the United States between 1860 and 1870, the photographer William Henry Jackson immortalized the Native American tribes of Nebraska and the territories of the American Wild West before the rapid advance of the newly constructed railways reached them. In Paris in 1910, Albert Kahn put together his *Archives of the Planet*, intended to capture 'aspects, practices and modes of human activity whose fatal disappearance is no more than a matter of time'.

At the same time the number of exhibitions devoted to photography multiplied, spreading images of the world and new ideas among a broad public. And around 1900, when the success of the Kodak camera was widely established, it seemed that anyone could appropriate Nature, it had become so ordinary. Freed from the frame and from a studio setting, the photograph became an expression of memory, both collective and individual. It was the reign of the souvenir photo, the time of collecting family portraits and holiday snapshots. But the vogue for the souvenir also affected the professionals, who had to relaunch their activities now that they were threatened by the Kodak. If anyone could use a camera at the 'press of a button', not everyone could take a good photograph – far from it. And there was something missing from these amateur pictures . . . what was it? Colour, of course: colour, which

(opposite left) Persian family, Tehran. This very rare image is the only remaining example of a photochrome of Iran from this period.
(opposite right) Bosnian nobleman on horseback
(right) View of Happy Valley, Llandudno

preserves the dream and stirs the memory long after the journey is over.

The invention of the Photochrome

At the end of the nineteenth century, colour photography had already been the subject of much research. For example, in France in 1868, Charles Cros and Louis Ducos du Hauron both independently discovered a way of taking pictures in trichrome, but it was still too complex for commercial use. In Switzerland, Orell Füssli belonged to a group of enthusiasts who always wanted to explore their art more deeply. Descended from a long line of Zurich printers, Füssli had worked since 1880 on a process that combined photography and lithography (he understood both techniques vey well), allowing a colour image to be reproduced from a black-and-white negative. For ten years he applied all his talents as a printer and colourist to completing his invention, the 'photochrome'. At last, in 1889, it was done. And it was a revelation.

The shining whiteness of snow, the dark green of the German forests, the stone of castles, the luminous shores of the Italian lakes, flowers, countless sunsets and captured moonlight – all these appeared, on the surface of the paper, in their original beauty. In addition there were portraits: shopkeepers, pedlars, men, women and children from all around the globe, represented with a stunning attention to detail. The photochrome gave the spectator a pleasure he or she had never experienced before. Presented at the Paris Exposition Universelle in 1900, Füssli's invention won first prize. His success was assured.

Photochromes by Photoglob (the company created by Füssli in Zurich to market his invention commercially) were sold at all the principal sites and holiday resorts in Europe, since it was tourists who bought them. They adored these views, with their clear, delicate colours that were so much more evocative than the painted or coloured postcards that had existed up until then. They brought back these new images from their travels, either loose or in frames, and showed them off proudly on their return; or else they ordered souvenir albums to be compiled on themes of their choosing: views of Egypt, the Holy Land or Constantinople; of Naples, Venice, the Swiss Alps or the Riviera; the Rhine, the Danube, the Ganges at Benares . . . In addition, a second line of photochromes reproduced works by the Old Masters, among which were Leonardo's *Last Supper*, Greuze's *The Broken Jug*, Raphael's *Donna Velata*, Millet's *Angelus*, or Rubens's *Three Graces* – paintings that one had admired in museums in the course of one's travels. This series was an enormous success, since the photochrome reproduced the masterpieces down to the last detail. Finally, at the turn of the twentieth century, the Niagara Falls, steamboats on the Mississippi, the Grand Canyon, Yellowstone Park, the Flatiron Building and the

streets of New York all joined the long list of images produced by Photoglob.

Such a range depended on the fact that Photoglob used negatives from all manner of sources: one could find Welsh landscapes by Frith, a portrait of a woman or a merchant in Cairo by Bonfils, or a view of Venice taken by Naya. A 1901 register of the Zurich company lists the assignments passed on to photographers working in Switzerland, Germany and all over Europe; there appear the names of the Frenchman Richard (inventor of the 'verascope', whose collection today forms part of the Hachette picture library), the Germans Müller, Werner, Schensky, and Emil Terschak, who covered the states of Austro-Hungary, the southern Alps and the Dolomites. But since copyright legislation did not require the publisher to mention photographers' names, most of the pictures cannot be properly attributed. No one knows how many photochromes were produced, nor how many prints were made from each negative.

The photochrome in America

As the Swiss distributed the photochrome in Europe – opening bases in London and Berlin, for example – American photographers became extremely interested in the new process. One of them, the Californian Edwin H. Husher, persuaded William Livingstone, the director of the powerful Detroit Photographic Company, to travel to Zurich to negotiate for an exclusive licence to distribute photochromes in North America.

The terms were agreed in 1896. The same year, the Detroit Photographic Company took on a former apprentice of Orell Füssli's, Albert Schuler, who was appointed director of the photochrome studio. Two years later, Husher invited his colleague and friend William Henry Jackson, the famous photographer, to come to Detroit. Jackson, who had 'skimmed' the American territories for thirty years, returned from a round-the-world trip, bringing with him more than 10,000 negatives. Most were views of North America, but the collection also included views of Europe, North Africa and Asia, notably of India. A draughtsman, set-painter, retoucher and fine art colourist turned photographer, Jackson was bowled over by photochromes. Having spent all his life looking for different ways of rendering his photographs in colour, what he saw before his eyes was nothing less than miraculous. Once processed using the photochrome technique, Jackson's negatives revealed a rich body of colour images – views of the Rockies and virgin American territories, and portraits of the Osage, Oto, Pawnee and Omaha tribes whom Jackson had encountered in 1867 when he was working in Nebraska with his brother, Ed.

The Detroit Photographic Company employed about forty artisans and a dozen or so salesmen. It produced, in good years, seven million

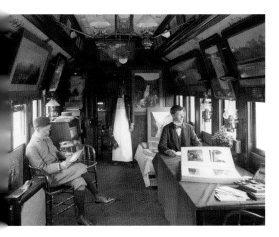

(far left) The personal carriage of William Livingstone, founder of the Detroit Photographic Company, which distributed the Photochrom process in the United States from 1896 onwards. Print from the Henry Ford Collection, Dearborn, Michigan

(left) Portrait of Paupuk Keewis, chief of the Iroquois tribe

photochromes. And, like Photoglob in Europe, the Detroit Photographic Company also used the photochrome process to print postcards, a potentially huge area of the market. William Henry Jackson is known to have been a director of the Detroit Photographic Company until the company collapsed in 1924. When it went bankrupt, thousands of photochromes became 'seized assets', and were found again by chance in an old warehouse in Bozeman, a town in the farthest reaches of Montana.

Photochromes around the world

The present directors of Photoglob Zurich believe that the photochrome disappeared shortly after the First World War, in about 1920. The thirtieth edition of their catalogue, from 1911, comprises some 30,000 pictures. Needless to say, it was somewhat difficult to select 300 images for this book. While some countries are heavily represented – England, Switzerland, Germany and nations that once belonged to the Austro-Hungarian empire – others have suffered from more or less total exclusion.

There are, for example, no photochromes of South America, with the exception of four or five good plates of Buenos Aires; none from Africa as a whole, save for North Africa and Egypt, which are widely covered; nor are there any from Japan. This patchy coverage is explained by the photochrome's

primary function as a photo souvenir, aimed principally at the traveller. So it is that most images show destinations that were popular with tourists between 1890 and 1914. In the case of Japan, the market was already well served by a plentiful supply of locally produced coloured photos.

The Austro-Hungarian empire occupies a prominent place in this book. A vast and magnificent territory, before 1914 it stretched from the Danube in the Carpathians to the Black Sea and the Adriatic coast, enclosing the Dolomites, the Dalmatian coast (now Croatia), Bosnia and Herzegovina, the former Czechoslovakia, Hungary and part of Poland.

The three hundred images selected here represent a typical cross-section of photochromes. Strong blues and bright colours are employed for southern countries, and tormented, dark, storm-bearing skies for those of the north. And the further one travels to the east, the more one notices that the colourists have made a particular attempt to emphasize the landscapes' exotic character and the luxuriance of the vegetation. What appears in these pages is a truly chromatic universe – the memory of a world that was lost but has been found once more.

England and Wales

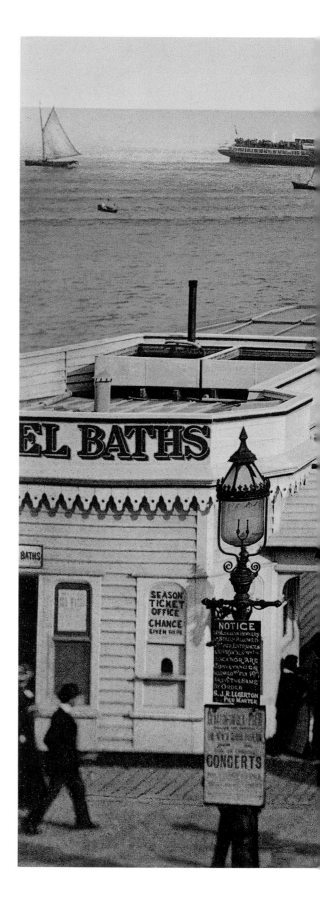

Clacton-on-Sea, the pier

The proliferation of piers in England during the Victorian era was truly an amazing phenomenon. There are jetties along coasts all over the world; but it was British engineers who turned them into places of leisure, offering the public various attractions at a price. Despite the modest admission fee – one penny at Clacton – piers were successful, and residents quickly understood where their interests lay. In the 1900s about one hundred piers dotted the English coast; fifty or so survive, which the National Piers Society, founded by Sir John Betjeman in 1979, aims to preserve. Clacton Pier, opened in 1871, is the work of Peter Schuyler Bruff, an engineer working for the Eastern Union Railway. Vessels of the Belle Steamer Company plied their trade here, and in 1882 the train brought the first summer day trippers from London. Finally, in 1893 the pier was given an octagonal pier-head in tarred pitch pine, with a Regency-style pavilion, concert hall, refreshment rooms and a waiting-room.

Hastings, yachts leaving harbour

Long before it became a seaside resort Hastings
was a port, one of the oldest in the whole country.
The inhabitants of this small Sussex town made
their living from fishing and smuggling. They
knew how to build boats that were solid enough
to withstand the strong southwesterly winds and
fast enough to evade the attentions of customs
officers. The *Bonaventure*, which distinguished
herself against the Spanish Armada, was launched
from the Hastings shipyards. Some time around the
middle of the nineteenth century, yachting, a less
risky and more aristocratic sport, established itself
all along the Sussex coast, stretching from Hastings
as far as Portsmouth, Hampshire and the Isle of
Wight beyond. At the turn of the twentieth century,
yachts leaving port were a very popular attraction.
At Hastings Yachting Club a magnificent pleasure
craft called the *Albertine* is still remembered: every
time she was launched, she drew a large crowd that
gathered on the seafront by the Queen's Hotel.

Rough seas at Bognor Regis

In 1787 a former hatter from Charing Cross named Sir Richard Hotham, who had made his fortune as a merchant with the East India Company, moved to Bognor in Sussex, where he set about developing the town as a resort. He dreamed of attracting George III, the Prince of Wales and the aristocracy who were frequent visitors to the fashionable town of Brighton further along the coast. Yet despite Sir Richard's efforts, the great and the good remained faithful to Brighton, and it was not until 1929 that King George V and Queen Mary honoured Bognor with their presence. The king bestowed the title 'Regis' on the town, which would have delighted its founder, and it began to flourish as a resort. Early guidebooks of the twentieth century describe Bognor as having 'an ideal beach for families with children' (presumably the weather was not always so fierce). On stormy days, the sea crashes against the rocks, and here one can enjoy the Turneresque colours of the lashing waves.

Portsmouth Harbour

Well sheltered by Spithead, and positioned on a
stretch of land that separates the Hampshire coast
from the Isle of Wight, Portsmouth has been the
Royal Navy's principal base and royal dockyard since
the sixteenth century. It was from Portsmouth that
Admiral Nelson set sail on the *Victory*, in 1805, to
fight in the Battle of Trafalgar against the Franco-
Spanish fleet. Some years later Charles Dickens was
born in Portsmouth (his father worked in the naval
dockyards): one of his childhood houses overlooks
the docks, and the young Charles spent many hours
at the garden gate watching the comings and goings
of the sailors. These memories would resurface in
his novels, most notably in *Nicholas Nickleby*, where
Mr Micawber and Mr Dorrit seem to share elements
of his father's character. Traces of Dickens and the
Victory can still be found in Portsmouth: the house
on Commercial Road where the writer lived after his
marriage has become the Dickens Museum, while
No. 2 dry dock is the home of the *Victory*, which has
been restored several times.

Salisbury Plain, Stonehenge

'Wiltshire, where huge open spaces spread out one
after the other, is a paradise for horse riders in times
of peace, and in times of war a vast field for military
manoeuvres' (quote from a 1947 guidebook). But
before it was a deserted stretch of military land,
Salisbury Plain was a region inhabited by many
people, who made their living by raising sheep and
from the wool trade, protected from invasion by
impenetrable forests. Even earlier, two and a half
thousand years before the birth of Christ, the men
of Salisbury Plain raised this field of stones.
Dominating the plain, Stonehenge was surrounded
by a raised-earth enclosure in the centre of which
stood thirty 5-metre (16-foot) monoliths. In this view
of the site, taken at the turn of the twentieth century,
some twenty or so stones can be seen still standing,
including three trilithons (three-stone structures).
The big leaning monolith right of centre measures
more than 7 metres (23 feet).

London, Tower Bridge

By the walls of the Tower of London, carriages await the return of people out for a walk. Right in the middle of the old city, Tower Hill offers an unimpeded view over the Thames, Tower Bridge and the Tower itself. The heart of the capital is here, at the White Tower, the impregnable fortress that William the Conqueror built to protect the city he had just conquered, and which was later to be enclosed within wider fortifications. Right on the edge of the river, 'full of jewels and dried blood, it has stifled the sighs of prisoners, the heavy sound of the falling bodies of Scottish rebels . . . it opens at water level, ready to take in the river as through a hippopotamus's open jaws' (Paul Morand). It was a royal residence as well as a prison, of course – and performed both roles at once during the reign of Henry III. The Tower houses the Crown Jewels of England, including those of the Black Prince, and jewels that Queen Victoria received from her British empire, 'from Burmese rubies and Cape diamonds, to Indian pearls and Australian sapphires'.

London, Cheapside

Let us glide over the statue of Sir Robert Peel in the foreground, and dive down into Cheapside, this ancient district of silk merchants, drapers and haberdashers, and powerful guilds, firmly established at the edges of the thriving and industrious City of London. In 1900 people travelled up and down Cheapside by coach and horses or on horse-drawn omnibuses, which competed with pedestrians who stepped off the crowded pavements. From his plinth, Sir Robert Peel looks down impassively as a policeman converses with two gentlemen at the foot of a street lamp: this 'bobby' is obliged to him both for his name and his job, since it was Robert ('Bobby') Peel's initiative that led to the formation of the London Metropolitan Police in 1829.

Robin Hood's Bay

A few miles from the famous Whitby Abbey, on the coast of 'indomitable Yorkshire', the village of Robin Hood's Bay is laid out on rocky ground, a cluster of hardy fishermen's houses with red-tiled roofs crammed closely together. Battered by the North Sea, the ramparts at the foot of the cliff evoke the time of the Viking invasions and the Norman Conquest. Robin Hood's Bay takes its name from a legend claiming that the outlaw of Sherwood Forest moored his boats here. There are in fact underground hiding places in the village, in which fishermen stored the goods that they brought back as contraband – the isolated position of Robin Hood's Bay has always lent itself to smuggling, made all the more easy by the fact that the tide goes out a long way, allowing boats to rest high and dry and men to bring their booty ashore on foot.

Fisher-girl from Cullercoats, Northumberland

This sturdy young woman – fresh-faced, fair of complexion, and a descendant of the Celts – comes from Northumberland, the northernmost bastion of Roman Britain before one arrives at the Scottish territories that Hadrian's soldiers never managed to penetrate. This 'country of coal and ships, castles and rivers that flow down from the solitude of the moors to the hustle and bustle of the sea ports' is cut in two by Hadrian's Wall, which from the Irish Sea to the North Sea has marked the border between Scotland and England since the year AD 122. Cullercoats, at the extreme eastern end of the wall, was founded in 1682, its people making their living from coal and the sale of sea salt. These two activities were closely linked – the coal was needed to heat the pans of seawater from which the salt crystals were collected – but collapsed at the turn of the eighteenth century and the inhabitants of Cullercoats returned to their fishing boats and nets. The census of 1861 lists 600 inhabitants, of which 156 were fishermen, 16 fisherwomen, 6 coastguards, 1 coastguard's widow, 18 sailors, 25 employees of the local brewery, and 1 miner. But twenty years later, after the arrival of the Blyth and Tyne railway line, the population had risen to 2,000 residents, 'including many visitors'. The time had come for the salt baths of Cullercoats.

Aberystwyth, Devil's Bridge

Situated on the rocky coast of Cardigan, Aberystwyth is a university town, a port and, since the nineteenth century, a lively seaside resort – the 'Biarritz of Wales', according to some guidebooks. About 20 kilometres (12 miles) separate Aberystwyth from Pont-ar-Mynach (Devil's Bridge), which since the 1890s can be reached by a railway that runs along the picturesque wooded Vale of Rheidol. After arriving at the station, it is only a few steps down to the bottom of the gorge. Devil's Bridge was built by monks in the twelfth century above the river Mynach, a raging torrent that runs between the sheer, rocky sides of the gorge; a new arch was added in the eighteenth century, and the structure was crowned in 1901 by an iron viaduct.

Penzance, St Michael's Mount

This strange little islet, perched like a hat or a seashell on an emerald sea, is St Michael's Mount – a counterpart to Normandy's Mont Saint-Michel, but in Cornwall. A causeway some half a mile long links it at low tide to the town of Marazion, near Penzance, whose roofs can be seen in the foreground. At high tide the Mount re-establishes its independence, retrenching behind its ramparts in the middle of the bay. Like its Normandy namesake, St Michael's Mount has a monastery, and it has been a site of pilgrimage ever since the fifth century, when St Michael appeared to a fisherman walking on the water (or standing at the tip of the promontory, according to other sources). More prosaically, St Michael's Mount was captured by the French Crown after the Norman Conquest and put under the administration of Mont Saint-Michel. Since the eighteenth century the castle and the abbey have belonged to the St Aubyn family, which rebuilt the ruins of the first church after it had been destroyed in an earthquake.

Lake District, Windermere

On Windermere, in the beautiful region of
the Cumbrian fells – the 'English Alps' – a coach
and horses drifts along on a steam-powered ferry,
which transports tourists from bank to bank during
the holiday season. The Lake District, an area of
solitude, peaks and green hills, was the destination
of choice in the nineteenth century for those
Romantic figures who became known as 'the Lake
Poets': Coleridge, Wordsworth and Southey. All
three lived by the lakes, experiencing days of ever-
changing rain and sunshine that encouraged them
in their meditations and cradled them in melancholy
periods of reverie. But the Lake District's mists fed
the collective imagination, and the folk tradition is
rich with diverting tales, such as the legend of the
white horse whose ghost, wandering across the
water from shore to shore, is a presage of bad luck.
Or the tale of the Tizzie-Wizzie, a water-loving beast
that has the body of a hedgehog, the tail of a squirrel
and the wings of a bee!

Isle of Man, the Laxey Wheel

A stone thrown into the Irish Sea, the Isle of Man
is one of the curiosities of the British Isles. First of
all, the Isle of Man has its own legislative assembly,
the Tynwald, comprising the Legislative Council
and the House of Keys, and its own Lieutenant-
Governor, who represents the Crown. It is also –
a matter of worldwide fame – the country where
the tailless Manx cat originates. Finally, it has the
'Lady Isabella', the superb Laxey Wheel, named
after the wife of the governor who inaugurated it
in 1854. Built by the engineer Robert Casement
to pump water from the mines of Glen Moar, Lady
Isabella – 22 metres (72 feet) in diameter – once
pumped more than 1,000 litres (250 gallons) of
water a minute. When the site closed in 1929,
the Laxey Wheel was purchased by Mr Edwin
Kneale, who had the good idea of maintaining it
and making it into a tourist attraction. The Isle of
Man's government took over the responsibility in
1965. In the words of a popular song, 'The Laxey
Wheel keeps turning, turning, turning / In Lady
Isabella's memory'.

Scotland

The return of the flock

A pale-blue sky announces the end of the day and bathes
the sombre colours of the Scottish moor in its light. The eye
follows the white flock as it winds its way to the top of the hill
and towards the last bend in the road. Leaving the sheep on their
peaceful crusade, the eye returns to the foreground and makes
out the trio of the shepherd and his two dogs. Confident that the
sheep are in safe care, one can take in the landscape, which the
photochrome technique paints so beautifully. Could one imagine
a scene like this without colour? The whole range of greens,
browns and yellows is explored, even the mauve pink of the
sunset that will soon tint the whole horizon.

Loch Awe, Kilchurn Castle

Abandoned two hundred and fifty years ago,
the solitary ruins of Kilchurn Castle are reflected in
the waters of Loch Awe, in the south-west Highlands.
It was in 1450 that Colin Campbell, first Lord of
Glenorchy, had it built. A five-storey tower house
with a courtyard defended by an outer wall, Kilchurn
originally occupied fully half of the island on which
it was constructed, which today has become a
peninsula (the loch was dredged in 1817 and the
water level dropped). In the seventeenth century
Sir John Campbell made plans to turn Kilchurn into
a garrison in order to house the troops of William
of Orange, husband of the new Queen of England.
But the government chose Fort William as its
base instead, and Sir John's plans came to nothing.
In 1740 the Campbells left Kilchurn to look after
their Perthshire estates, moving to Taymouth in the
east of Scotland. The deserted Kilchurn Castle was
struck by lightning in 1760 and was never raised
from its ruins.

Dumfries, The Sands

A sturdy market town of robust red sandstone houses, in 1900 Dumfries lived from the riches that came from its river, the Nith. In the south-west of the Lowlands, tucked in at the end of a vast marshy estuary, the town is a prosperous agricultural centre where regular cattle fairs take place. The region's farmers are seen here, who have come with their herds and are waiting for buyers (how surprised they would be to see the skateboard park that has recently been built on this spot). Today Dumfries lives off tourism, notably the cult devoted to the memory of Robbie Burns, the most popular of all Scottish poets; a 'Burns circuit' guides visitors to the places that 'Rabbie' used to frequent, the inns where he composed his ballads, the farm where he lived, the house in which he died, the cemetery where he lies buried . . .

Ireland

Glengarriff, the view from Roche's Hotel

In the south-west of Ireland, from Cork to Macroom and Bantry,
the natural beauties of Killarney were extolled in numerous
guidebooks of the early twentieth century. One French writer,
Paul Morand, claimed enthusiastically: 'It was Eden!' And he
described in minute detail the luxuriant vegetation, the
abundance of parks with 'enormous rhododendrons filling the
undergrowth, perfect green rolling lawns, where cows the colour
of ebony lay sleeping'. By this time Glengarriff, in Bantry Bay, had
become a reputable tourist destination. Arriving from Cork via
the Prince of Wales' Way – named after Edward VII, who used it
in 1848 – is a route recommended as much by the guidebooks of
yesterday as those of today. Roche's Royal Hotel in Glengarriff
is, to judge by the evidence shown here, 'a hotel with a view' –
a wonderful vista to delight the eyes whatever the weather.

Dublin, Sackville Street

Capital of the Republic of Ireland, Dublin is a city
that the French writer Michel Déon described as
'incomprehensible to anyone who is not Irish'.
Torn by its struggles against English occupation
on the one hand, and by the conflict between its
two communities (an overwhelming majority of
Catholics and a minority of Protestants) on the
other, 'Dublin would be a city to fill your heart with
despair . . . a city that has shed an appalling amount
of blood for the sake of Irish freedom . . . where
poverty is made all the more striking by the
proximity of wealthier districts'. These wealthier
districts, before independence, were concentrated
around Sackville Street, where the grand hotels had
become established: the Imperial, the Metropole,
the Edinburgh. Sackville Street begins at the statue
to Daniel O'Connell (left in the foreground) and
crosses the Liffey at the bridge named after the same
man. O'Connell – called the Liberator – obliged the
British government to vote in the Act of Catholic
Emancipation in 1829. This victory did not stop
either British oppression or the blockade that
unleashed the terrible famine of the middle of the
nineteenth century, which affected Catholics and
Protestants alike and caused some two million

Irish to leave their country. 'I am leaving Dublin . . .
I am not despondent however for I know that even
if I fail to make my way such failure proves very
little. I shall try myself against the powers of the
world.' These words of farewell are those of James
Joyce, a writer of immense stature who set sail on
1 December 1902 and, through all his wanderings,
pursued his Irish dream.

An Irish colleen

'How sweet are thy Maidens / Oh, Land of the
Green!' With a big woollen shawl around her
shoulders, woven with a long fringe and dominated
by the colour green, here is a real young Irish girl.
Her brown hair has a fiery red to it and frames a
face of peachy skin, and she wears a headscarf
made of Indian printed cotton arranged over her
décolletage. Below the bodice she has tied a long
apron of traditional Irish linen around her waist.

Northern Ireland, Giant's Causeway

You would have to be a good walker to get to the
Giant's Causeway before the coast road was built in
1830. But the last stop would be at Bushmills, whose
famous whiskey would give the more faint-hearted
tourists a little courage. And what a spectacle this
chaotic scene makes, with the great basalt columns
rearing up one against the other, leading in serried
ranks down to the sea where they disappear. Forty
thousand columns, appearing as if they had been
forced up by centuries of waves, are the remains of
a lava field whose fragments slowly fused together,
making these fantastic blocks. But if you have a
fondness for legends, you may prefer to believe the
one in which Finn McCool – Finn the Giant, who
was the commander of the king of Ireland's armies –
made this causeway for his own use, to reach his
betrothed in the isles of the Hebrides.

Carrick-a-Rede and the Larrybane Cliffs

Continuing eastwards from the Giant's Causeway
along the coastal road, the traveller arrives at the bay
of Larrybane, where a breathtaking view awaits:
strung across a gap of over 25 metres (82 feet), an
unlikely-seeming rope bridge links the edge of the
cliff to the little island of Carrick-a-Rede (Gaelic for
'the rock on the road'). It was fishermen who erected
this precarious-looking structure in the nineteenth
century, in order to throw their nets across the
narrow passage through which salmon swim during
the migrating season. Each year, from April to
September, the ritual continues to be performed,
and tourists are cordially invited to cross the bridge
to help with the fishing. Those who are tempted
by the sound of this expedition should remember
that they would do well to leave their dogs in the car
park, if one is to believe the nineteenth-century tales
of more than one fisherman who has looked on
helplessly as his four-legged friend was blown off
the bridge by a gust of wind.

The Netherlands

Amsterdam, Oudezijds Achterburgwal

Any town that has 'streets of water' is likely to be compared with Venice. Such is the case with Amsterdam, Rotterdam, and plenty of other towns in the Netherlands and Northern Europe. This canal, lined with tall houses overlooking the water on one side and a narrow street on the other, is in the oldest district of Amsterdam, Oudezijds Achterburgwal. Traditionally frequented by sailors, today the area is known as a red-light district (neon lights advertise to passers-by the shop windows where prostitutes wait for customers).

Rotterdam, Coolvest and the De Hoop windmill

Before 1900 the Coolvest district was one of the most 'authentic' in the city. Big barges moved up and down the canal, whose still waters stagnated between two quaysides planted with trees. Red-brick houses with crow-stepped gables look down onto the water, and horse-drawn carriages passed beneath their windows. At the end of the canal turn the sails of the De Hoop windmill, with their 'black veins' that Théophile Gautier compared to 'the wings of a dragonfly magnified thousands of times by solar microscope'. In the 1920s, at the instigation of Rotterdam's Mayor Zimmerman, the canal was filled in and covered by a metropolitan street, and Coolvest became Coolsingel.

Scheveningen, the beach and casino

Up until the early years of the nineteenth century, Scheveningen was a peaceful village of fishermen where painters used to come and pitch their easels (the sky over Scheveningen and its flat-bottomed barges have been painted many times by Flemish artists). In 1818 the fashion for sea bathing prompted a certain Jacob Pronk to set up a small spa building on the sands that dominated the beach. In the beginning it was no more than a plank construction with four cabins for the use of bathers, but in 1824 it obtained the status of a municipal establishment. The construction of a new road between Scheveningen and The Hague at around the same time encouraged the development of the resort, which went from strength to strength. One of the first hotel-casinos opened in 1885. Devastated by fire the following year, it was rebuilt and ultimately expanded still further.

Utrecht, the Oudegracht and the Bakkerbrug Bridge

This photochrome of Utrecht calls to mind the archetypal Dutch scene evoked by Théophile Gautier: 'It is a view of any city in Holland: red-brick walls, trees, an arched bridge, a bell tower or belfry rising above the roofs of the houses, a canal with a quay in the foreground of the picture.' Everything is there: the Oudegracht, the Bakkerbrug Bridge and, dominating the scene in the background, the belfry of St Catherine's Church.

Dordrecht, the Voorstraatshaven

Situated at the meeting of three rivers, the modern-day city of Dordrecht still bears the imprint of its rich past as a port. Here, history becomes tangible. The historic heart of Dordrecht is the Voorstraatshaven district, whose streets are paved with red brick and alive with busy shops. In 1900 Voorstraatshaven (literally 'street at the fore-port') was nothing but a stretch of water lined with houses with gabled roofs, an emerald canal between sky and stones. The uncompleted tower of the Grote Kerke (Great Church) rears up behind the houses, scraping the clouds.

Fisherfolk on Marken Island

Here is a typical Dutch landscape: the ancient
Marken Island. Initially on a peninsula, the village
of Marken was detached from the mainland in the
eighteenth century by a violent storm that divided it
from the coast by more than 2 kilometres (1¼ miles).
It was not until 1957 that the island was reconnected
with the mainland by means of a dike. In 1900
Marken was a small port that lived off fishing.
On the banks, raised barely a few centimetres above
the water for protection from the waves that easily
swamped the land during rough weather, the
fishermen's families lived in wooden houses built
on stilts. Men, women and children would dress in
bright colours, and the Marken style of dress (see
opposite) still forms a part of the local folk tradition –
it is said that some unreconstructed types refuse to
wear off-the-peg clothes even today. The pale colours
of a Dutch sky in springtime, and the unencumbered
horizon, envelop this flat landscape, where even so
much as the hull of a barge or the posts of a fence
stand out in relief.

Belgium

View of Antwerp

The eye is drawn to the angle formed by the rows of gabled roofs in the foreground, then passes over the dark blue of the roofs and the bell towers to the light blue of the river Scheldt. The long row of bristling cranes on the riverbank hint at the location of the port, which has been the source of Antwerp's wealth since the time of Rubens and the Holy Roman Emperor Charles V. Continuing along the line of the river, the viewer's attention is absorbed by the polders (reclaimed land protected by dikes) and travels on to the lowlands of eastern Flanders and the pale blue and green horizon beyond.

Brussels, the Grand-Place

On the Grand-Place in Brussels, one of the most
celebrated examples of Italo-Flemish architecture
in Belgium, stand the principal guildhalls: the
boatmen, haberdashers, archers, printers and
booksellers, and so on. One can identify the House
of the Swan (symbol of the butchers' guild) by its
gable on which is mounted the fine figure of the bird
with its wings outstretched. In front of the wealthy
façades open-air markets are held daily, where the
scent of flowers mixes with the smells of delicacies.
People selling hard-boiled eggs or *couques* (dry
pastries) walk among the oak tables of the taverns,
which overflow with plain-speaking beer-drinkers.

Brussels, the Galeries Saint-Hubert

A group of people are strolling through the
unusually deserted Passage Saint-Hubert at their
leisure. Opened in 1847 by King Leopold I, these
fine galleries were designed by the Flemish architect
Jean-Pierre Cluysenaer. The Palladian columns, the
arcades with their pilastered arcades, and the statues
mounted in their niches all evoke Renaissance Italy.
Barely had the arcade opened when it achieved great
success and aroused considerable excitement. The
newspaper *La Chronique*, the Théâtre des Galeries
Saint-Hubert (1847) and the Théâtre Vaudeville
(1884), the confectioner Jean Neuhaus (1857), and
even the Café de la Renaissance took up residence
here. A great meeting place for artistic and literary
circles, the Café (today's Taverne du Passage) played
host to many men of letters, from Victor Hugo and
Baudelaire to Apollinaire, Verlaine and Rimbaud.

Ghent, the church of St Nicholas, the town hall and the church of St Bavo

At the confluence of four rivers – the Lys, the Scheldt, the Liève and the Moer – Ghent is built on no fewer than twenty-six islands that are linked together by a hundred or so bridges. The old capital of Flanders is rich in monuments: the tower of St Nicholas, the oldest church in Ghent, rises from the fortress (shown here in the foreground) above the grain market. Beyond, we can see the Belfry, symbol of communal freedoms, on top of which a dragon spreads its brass and gold wings; and in the very background the outline of the cathedral of St Bavo. 'View from the top of St Bavo . . . and one has to climb 450 steps to get there. Ghent is laid out in a Gothic configuration almost as well preserved as that of Antwerp', noted Victor Hugo. He also visited the crypt, 'a fine and noble subterranean place' where Van Eyck is buried, and in the church he admired the brass candlesticks rescued from London's St Paul's Cathedral at the time of the Great Fire. Hugo concluded: 'Their cathedral is burnt, their master is dead . . . but these have remained because they are beautiful and one notices only their beauty: history passes on, art remains.'

Bruges, the Béguinage Bridge and the spire of Notre-Dame

The decadent writer J.-K. Huysmans once said of Bruges that it is 'a delicious city, both mystical and demonic at the same time, puerile and serious'. Here, the visitor may wander along the shady walks by the old ramparts, drift this way and that along the streets and canals while the forty-eight bells of Notre-Dame ring out. In this cool-coloured photochrome, the narrow spire of Notre-Dame rises up behind the gabled roof of a fine red-brick house that looks out over the Place de la Vigne. The pretty three-arched bridge leading to the recluses of the Béguinage, the children playing happily by the canal, the elegant gentleman out for a walk who looks back at us – all complete a bucolic picture.

France

Paris, the Big Wheel

The twin sister of the Big Wheel designed in 1893 by George Washington Gale Ferris for the Chicago World's Fair, the Big Wheel for the 1900 Paris Exposition Universelle could lift 1,200 high-flying enthusiasts at once, squeezed into 40 little compartments. One complete turn of the wheel would last about an hour – with a stop at the top, from where the passengers could look down on the Exposition some 100 metres (330 feet) below. The presence of the Big Wheel on the Avenue Suffren, close to the Eiffel Tower, is rather ironic when one considers that the American model was actually designed with the express intention of competing with Gustave Eiffel's work. The unfortunate Ferris – who died in misery in 1896 – never witnessed either the opening or the demolition of his Big Wheel in 1937, to which no one in America paid the least attention.

Mers-les-Bains and Le Tréport

With its lovely brick-and-stone villas laid out in
terraces along the chalky cliff, Le Tréport – with its
beach, Mers-les-Bains – was a very popular seaside
resort during the Belle Epoque: 'pleasure trains'
brought trippers from Paris at the end of every week.
The peaceful little fishing port of which Victor Hugo
had been so fond in the 1830s had changed a good
deal: according to a contemporary diarist in the
1900s, the beach now comprised 'almost as many
bathers as pebbles'. And yet the view from the upper
town remains lovely. Here, the eye ranges freely
from the rooftops (more Flemish than Norman)
along the pale beach all the way to the headland.
Writing of the seemingly infinite horizon, Hugo
wrote: 'Oh! That is where one can feel the beating
of wings. If I didn't have my nest in Paris I would
rush there!'

Calais, the Hôtel de Guise

Little remains of the Calais of the Middle Ages,
which belonged to the English Crown for two
hundred years. At the beginning of the Rue Royale,
this gateway flanked by turrets – baptized the Hôtel
de Guise in honour of François de Guise, who retook
the city in 1558 – is in fact a vestige of the merchants'
exchange, constructed at the end of the fourteenth
century in the English Gothic style. Despite such
political upheavals, it is to England's proximity that
Calais owes its prosperity: the new port, opened in
1889 and flanked by a jetty more than 1 kilometre
(¹/₂ mile) long, enabled steamers on the Calais–Dover
crossing to come alongside the quay in all weather
conditions.

Honfleur, the Lieutenancy

The American writer James Fenimore Cooper, who
visited France in 1833, was struck in Honfleur by
'the old and sombre masses of the buildings' that
recalled for him 'certain Flemish paintings'. While
finding such colours 'imposing and beautiful', this
tourist from the New World at first regretted the
lack of 'livelier shades [that] would have rendered
the view gayer and more pleasant'. Then, won over
once and for all, he declared that colour would suit
the architecture as badly as it would the countryside:
'a little custom has taught me that my taste had
corrupted me', he concluded. Solidly planted on
the quayside at Honfleur, the old sixteenth-century
Lieutenancy sets its dark and imposing mass against
the clear sky. Horse-drawn carriages and a few
people on quayside bring the scene to life.

Trouville, the promenade and the Grand Salon

During the Belle Epoque, a small steamer shuttled back and forth between Honfleur and Trouville, bringing tourists in search of amusement to the 'queen of all Calvados's beaches'. More popular than Deauville, its neighbour and great rival, Trouville was in 1900 the most visited seaside resort on the Normandy coast. Two casinos, two big bathing establishments, a theatre, tennis courts, and hotels of every category attracted thousands of trippers during the high season. On his *Voyage d'un petit Parisien à la mer* ('Journey of a Little Parisian to the Seaside', 1898), Constant de Tours, author of several guidebooks to the French coasts, described the promenade that passed in front of the big hotels: 'When one sees this crowd of bathers in various bright colours walking in groups, mingling and passing each other in opposite directions, one is brought to mind of a kaleidoscope of many colours turning continuously.'

Saint-Malo, the beach at low tide

At Saint-Malo – a city enclosed by ramparts that
Flaubert compared to a 'crown of stones set on the
waves' – the rocks encircling the jetty at low tide
mark out 'a thousand granite baths'. On a hot
summer's day in 1835, Hugo, who hated the
fortifications and the citadel but loved the sea,
threw himself happily into these hollows filled with
water, delighted to be 'shaken up in the foamy waves',
which sent him 'backwards on to those diabolical
pointed rocks about ten times over'. Sixty years later,
on the same beach, some less adventurous bathers
enjoy their stay in Saint-Malo. During the Belle
Epoque Saint-Malo was a renowned seaside resort,
where good hotels welcomed a well-to-do family
clientele. The Franklin (on the left in this
photochrome), a luxury establishment next to the
Casino, was built on the Sillon – the road on the
isthmus that provided the only link between the
town and dry land before the creation of the dikes.

Nantes, confluence of the Erdre and the Loire

The old capital of the Duchy of Brittany, Nantes is a
severe, ambitious city, a rebel against a tormented
past. This unusual view of Nantes is taken from the
Isle of Feydeau, at a time when the railway line from
Orléans passed through the heart of the city, linking
its two stations, the Gare d'Orléans and the Gare
de la Bourse. In an image of both serenity and
animation, the eye is drawn by the deep emerald of
the waters and then moves up to the pale, hazy sky,
in harmony with the blue slates that cover the roofs
of the white stone houses. On the left, the grey spire
of St Nicholas's Church rises up above the roofs, and,
entering from stage right, a locomotive unfurls its
banner of steam like white cotton wool.

Paris, the Château d'Eau at the Exposition Universelle, 1900 (overleaf)

Organized to mark the first year of the new century,
the fifth Exposition Universelle ('World's Fair') in
Paris was intended to be unforgettable. A moving
walkway – the first of its kind – ran between the
new Alexandre III Bridge and the site, offering a
panoramic view. This extraordinary photochrome
shows one of the most famous buildings of the
Exposition, a palace raised to the glory of Electricity –
'the religion of the twentieth century', as it has
been called – in front of which glittered the coloured
fountains of the Château d'Eau, lit by 5,000
incandescent bulbs. Set on the Champ de Mars,
at the heart of the Exposition, this thousand-and-
one-nights installation dazzled the crowds of people
who thronged around the pool, not wanting to
miss a single moment of the spectacle. Could one
think of a better souvenir of the Exposition than
this marvellous colour image, at a time when only
the photochrome was equal to the task of conveying
its grandeur?

Lyon, the banks of the Saône

Descriptions of Lyon written by travellers in the nineteenth century are contradictory, to say the least. The misery of the city in 1837 shocked Charles Dickens, who swore in future 'to make a detour of several miles to avoid coming across it again on his way' – and several years later Socialist writer and activist Flora Tristan wrote that here 'you must raise your head to see a patch of blue sky between two walls'. But Stendhal, who visited in the same year as Dickens, found that, as far as he could see, the city was 'very rich', and he spoke of it enthusiastically. One could eat very well here, even better than in Paris: he found 'twenty-two ways of preparing potatoes', of which a dozen were entirely original. Finally, in a letter to his son Lucien, the painter Camille Pissarro wrote in 1898 that, without being picturesque, 'Lyon is a big and beautiful city', and that 'the banks of the Saône are really beautiful'. From the evidence of this photochrome (dating to exactly the same period as Pissarro describes), with its beautiful summer light and the blue waters of the peaceful Saône, the viewer might be inclined to agree.

The railway viaduct at Le Fayet and a view of Mont Blanc

On a bright summer's day, three companions walk along the road lined with larch and fir trees that follows the Arve, the impetuous torrent that crosses the Chamonix valley. They seem dwarfed by their surroundings: the landscape is dominated by the enormous snowy mass of Mont Blanc, and by the seven arches of the Sainte-Marie viaduct across which a toy train is passing. A monumental work of engineering built in 1899 for the company PLM, the viaduct crosses the Arve, downhill from the station at Les Houches. From Saint-Gervais-Le Fayet, the line reached Chamonix in 1904, and the Swiss border in 1908. It remains in service to this day.

Marseille, the Quai de la Joliette and the Messageries Maritimes

'Here is the real gateway to the Orient!' exclaimed the Guatemalan traveller and writer Enrique Gomez Carrillo when he disembarked in Marseille in 1900. Walking through the port, where the whiff of tar mixed with the reek of garlic and the smells of eaux-de-vie from the bars, he evoked the ships leaving 'for the yellow seas, the merchants of the Asiatics selling rare spices, garish cloths and arousing perfumes'. Built during the Second Empire to accommodate steamships, the Quai de la Joliette was a place of intense activity in the nineteenth century. Passengers and goods of the Messageries Maritimes company embarked and disembarked at the Quai de la Joliette. Every race and nationality rubbed shoulders here, 'sailors from Scandinavia . . . calm and youthful Germans with eyes as blue as the waters of the gulf, people from the Levant with the profile of birds of prey, from Egypt, Tunisia, Tripoli . . .', making Marseille the most cosmopolitan, the most exotic of cities.

Marseille, the Corniche

The stretch of the Corniche between the Pharo and the Prado is one of the oldest promenades in Marseille. In 1900 one would go there on foot or by carriage, and dine at the grand hotel La Reserve, whose restaurant had a fine reputation, especially for its bouillabaisse (Stendhal, who was fond of a little extravagance, mentioned it in his 1837 *Mémoires d'un touriste*). Here it was as peaceful as the centre of town was busy, and the Corniche road skirted little creeks with fishermen's huts and brightly painted boats pulled up on the sand. Fine white houses were tucked away in the greenery, their fragrant gardens buzzing with cicadas. The Marseillais liked to come here at the end of the day to enjoy the cool evening air and to watch the sun set into the sea.

Grasse, the Porte-Neuve

Surrounded by olive trees, fig trees and fields
of roses, the little town of Grasse enjoys a very
particular climate, sheltered from cool breezes by
its mountainous environs. The hills that dominate
the town, with its profusion of narrow streets, give
it 'a completely Genoese physiognomy', as Stendhal
once remarked. But the comparison stops there,
since Stendhal deplored Grasse's 'utter lack of
architecture or cafés' and complained about the
heady smells of resin wafting from the perfumery.
Although the effluvia from the perfumery may have
been very much in evidence back in the nineteenth
century, Grasse today is one of the prettiest medieval
towns of all the Côte d'Azur. The Porte-Neuve opens
onto a maze of little streets, cool in summer, dotted
with fountains and covered by vaulted passages,
which the visitor feels compelled to explore.

Nice, the market

The county of Nice was officially annexed by France
in 1860, when the Treaty of Turin was signed by
Napoleon III and Cavour, the minister of the Italian
King Victor Emmanuel II. So it was that Nice
became a favourite destination for the upper middle
classes of the Second Empire, who followed the
emperor and empress, while the English and the
Russians had already established their winter
quarters here. In 1900 the rise of tourism and the
fashion for sea bathing turned Nice into a resort that
lived for the summer. Its hotels, the new casino-jetty
on the Promenade and its carnival attracted more
and more customers every year. But in 1900 Old
Nice was still much in evidence – craftsmen in the
side streets, garlic-sellers sitting by their doors,
open-air markets – and the town still had an Italian
feel to it.

Cannes and the monastery of Saint-Honorat

On the deserted shore where Napoleon landed
on his return from Elba, a man sits facing the
calm sea. On his right are the Isles of Lérin and the
monastery of Saint-Honorat – founded in 427 by the
Hungarian monk Honoratus, who landed here and,
by making the sign of the cross, banished at a stroke
not only all the snakes in the area but paganism too.
Chateaubriand came on a pilgrimage in 1838; and
the writer Prosper Mérimée, in his role as inspector
of historic monuments, visited the monastery
and asked for it to be repaired. The sister island
to Saint-Honorat, Sainte-Marguerite, was used as
a state prison: Napoleon's Mameluk soldiers were
locked up here, as well as (it is claimed) the Man
in the Iron Mask.

Bonifacio

The wild sentinel city of Bonifacio, protected by its
citadel, was reputed to be impregnable, yet it was
subjected to countless attacks over the centuries.
Occupied in turn by the Holy See, the Pisans
and the Genoese, the city fell to France in 1767,
two years before the birth of Napoleon Bonaparte.
The economist Adolphe Blanqui, who was
commissioned by the government of Louis-Philippe
in 1838 to draw up a report on the 'economic and
moral state of Corsica', was 'struck by the particular
physiognomy' of this vertiginous chalk promontory,
rising 70 metres (230 feet) above the Mediterranean
on the southernmost point of the island. The view
of this city, perched on a rocky spur eaten away
by the waves, is altogether captivating: the viewer
can all but hear the song of the sea at the foot of
the cliffs, the whistling of the wind and the cries
of the seagulls.

Switzerland

The Aletsch Glacier

At the feet of these two gentlemen, who appear to have stepped
from the pages of a novel by Jules Verne, the Aletsch Glacier
rolls past in frozen waves. Through his binoculars one of them
observes the prisms of white, green, violet and blue ice, colours
that change constantly in the sunlight; the other man rests his
hand on his stick and contemplates the silence of the mineral
ocean that lies before his eyes. Dominated by the peak of the
Aletsch, from which one of the main tributaries of the glacier
flows, the enormous Aletsch Glacier stretches for 25 kilometres
(15 miles). The old tourist guidebooks recommended a journey
there to admire the view, 'one of the most beautiful of the Swiss
Alps', from Eggishorn, a summit that can be reached by following
an old mule track from the resort of Flesch, crossing the forests
and pastures. For the last two hours of the excursion – which was
expected to last five hours in total – travellers were 'well advised
to employ the services of a mountain guide' to lead them through
the zigzagging rocky pathway.

Grindelwald, the Wetterhorn cable car

In the very heart of the Bernese Oberland, Grindelwald has been a famous mountaineering centre since the 1850s and a summer resort frequented by travellers, especially the English. Byron set the action of his epic poem *Manfred* here – named after a ruined castle in the Wilderswil forest – and the historian and theologian William Coolidge, another habitué of Grindelwald, is buried in the Protestant cemetery in the village. Grindelwald is known for its glacier, whose lower reaches in the nineteenth century came down as far as the first houses. In a century and a half the edge of this sea of ice has receded by almost 2 kilometres (over 1 mile), and today only a footbridge across the gorge shows the glacier's extent in times gone by. The Wetterhorn cable car, which first entered service in 1908, was built by a German named Feldman, maker of the suspended railway at Wuppertal, but the First World War brought activities to a halt. The Swiss Transport Museum in Lucerne has preserved one of the old cabins, with balcony, from this first cable car service.

The Schynige Platte Railway

The little rack-and-pinion Schynige Platte Railway dates from 1893. Amid breathtaking scenery, which takes in the three highest mountains in Switzerland – the Eiger, the Mönch and the Jungfrau – the train climbs for 7 kilometres (4½ miles) from Wilderswil to the summer belvedere, at an altitude of more than 2,000 metres (6,600 feet).

The Staubbach Falls

Wooden houses with wide roofs sheltering the windows beneath are tucked into the crook of the green valley of Lauterbrunnen. Behind them is the white cascade of the Staubbach Falls, looking 'exactly like falling smoke' (Victor Hugo). There is no horizon, but light shines through an opening at in the background and illuminates the bank of pink clouds.

The gorges of the Rosenlaui Glacier

Some of the most impressive natural sites in the Alps are to be found in the Meiringen area: the Aar Gorge, the Wildbach Gorges, the Reichenbach Falls, the sources of the Siebenbrunnen. . . . Carved out by the Rosenlaui Glacier, the Wildbach Gorges feature some 'considerable construction work – steps, tunnels, galleries, footbridges . . . all carried out with the greatest respect for nature,' as an old *Blue Guide* puts it. Visiting this mineral chaos is only possible only in the company of a guide. As one leaves the gorges, a thirty-minute walk along a steep path leads to a beautiful viewpoint over the Rosenlaui Glacier.

Panorama of Lucerne

'The lake, as blue as flaming sulphur,' wrote Leo Tolstoy in 1857, 'still, polished, convex, stretched out before the windows, broadened between the green banks . . . and, adopting a darker shade, collided and disappeared into the mountains, clouds and glaciers, piled up one after the other.' The lake's mirrored surface emphasizes the sharp, clear townscape of Lucerne, while the wooded hills behind rise up to the crenellated profiles of Mount Pilatus.

Territet, boats on Lake Geneva

Close to the fashionable town of Montreux, Territet is one of those villages dotted along the Swiss Riviera from Vevey to Chillon, with its villas, palaces and pleasure ports lining the banks of Lake Geneva. Since the beginning of the nineteenth century, the mild and even climate and the place's calm and beauty had made it one of the favoured retreats of the European aristocracy; but it was the opening of the Simplon railway line that launched it as a resort, and in 1861 the Orient Express stopped at Territet. In 1888 the Grand Hôtel des Alpes replaced the older, more modest Chasseur des Alpes. In February 1893 Elizabeth of Bavaria, Empress Consort of Austria (known as 'Sissi'), arrived at the Grand Hôtel for the first time. She returned to stay on many occasions, going for long walks alone around the lake and the surrounding countryside. On the 10 September 1898, returning from a visit to Baron Rothschild, Sissi was stabbed on the landing stage of the steamer *Genève* by an anarchist named Luigi Luccheni. The inhabitants of Territet raised a statue to the memory of their much-loved and illustrious guest in 1902, on the Place des Roses.

Mount Pilatus, the Esel approach

'The Pilatus, being a singular sort of giant, puts on his hat in fine weather, and takes it off when it rains.' This Lucernois saying illuminates the unusual weather patterns of Lucerne's neighbouring mountain: when the summit is crowned with a cloud, it is a sign of good weather, and when there is no cloud, it means rain. This phenomenon is easily explained by the presence of a lake at the top of the Pilatus, whose water – when warmed by the sun – creates the cloud. From Lucerne, a cogwheel railway, one of the steepest in the world, takes thirty minutes to reach the Pilatus-Kulm refuge. Hanging on to the steep sides of the Esel, the second-highest peak in the massif, the railway's final stretch features no fewer than four tunnels.

The Gornergrat Hotel and the Matterhorn

Zermatt – today a fashionable and expensive resort, although it is still referred to as 'the village' – is surrounded by the Matterhorn, the Monte Rosa and the Dent Blanche, all of which are over 4,000 metres (13,000 feet) high. Zermatt is also one of Europe's oldest mountaineering centres, since the Matterhorn remains a challenge for climbing aficionados. A rack-and-pinion railway leads from the village to the Kulm Hotel, a little below the Gornergrat; there, in complete tranquillity, the visitor can contemplate one of the most extraordinary panoramas in the whole of Switzerland. Guidebooks recommended climbing up to the Gornergrat on foot towards the end of the afternoon and waiting to watch the sunset.

The Diavolezza, by the Pers Glacier

The southernmost and largest of the Swiss
cantons, Graubünden benefits from exceptionally
high rates of sunshine, which encouraged the early
development of numerous resorts. Winter sports
are especially popular here: one thinks of St Moritz
in the district of Majola, and Pontresina in the Upper
Engadin – the centre for mountaineering courses in
the Bernina Range. A tour of the Diavolezza is one
of the classic excursions that tourists could embark
upon with a guide; the more faint-hearted would
be able to stop at the Boval Cabin, at the Diavolezza
Pass, from where the view over the Pers Glacier,
surrounded by snowy peaks, is one of the most
beautiful in all the Graubünden Alps.

A mountain guide

Standing solidly with his back to a precipice
and clutching his alpenstock, here is a mountain
guide who is larger than life. One can imagine him
walking with a sure and measured pace, amusing
visitors with tales of chamois hunters, foolish
travellers who fell into ravines, and caves inhabited
by spirits.

Austria

Zell-am-See and the Kitzsteinhorn

This image of a Tyrolean couple in a boat at Zell-am-See is pure nostalgia. In 1900 this little health resort at the foot of the snowy slopes of the Kitzsteinhorn and the Schmittenhöhe prospered during fine weather. In the summer the railway would bring city-dwellers in search of clean air and nature (the station was opened in 1875), principally from Salzburg or neighbouring Bavaria. Elisabeth of Bavaria, Empress Consort of Austria, did not like Bad-Ischl and came to Zell for the first time in 1885, while Emperor Franz Joseph joined her there in 1893. An excellent walker, Elisabeth liked to climb the Schmittenhöhe in order to admire the panorama over the great Austrian Alps.

Salzburg, the Pferdeschwemme

The very Catholic city of Salzburg, home to the
prince-archbishops of the Holy Roman Empire, has
been a centre for arts and music since the eighteenth
century. Its rich protectors, fervent admirers of
the Italian Renaissance, dreamed of turning their
state capital into a 'German Rome' and embellished
it accordingly. The old town, tucked between the
river and the Mönchsberg mountain, contains the
Residenz, the Franziskanerkirche, the Italianate
cathedral and several Baroque fountains – as well,
of course, as the Mozart Museum. The photochrome
here shows the Pferdeschwemme (the 'horse pond'),
built in 1695 in front of the old archbishops' stables
at the foot of the Mönchsberg. At the centre of this
oval basin is the 'Horse Tamer' by Bernhard Mändl.

Salzkammergut, the Hotel Schafberg

With its countless lakes, deep forests and
vertiginous peaks, the Salzkammergut is one of
the most picturesque regions of Austria. From
Salzburg to Bad-Ischl, its thermal resorts have
been popular with tourists every summer since
the beginning of the nineteenth century. In season,
the villages shake off their torpor, the villas of rich
Viennese open their shutters, motor boats carve
white trails across the lakes, and hoteliers await their
hungry guests returning from walks in the fresh air.
In the village of St Wolfgang, the Gasthof Weisses
Rössl, or White Horse Inn – made popular in 1930
by a famous operetta – was the sort of place where
visitors could enjoy dinner to the sound of Tyrolean
singing. In 1893 the Schafberg rack-and-pinion
railway was put into service. A few minutes' walk
from the station, on a rocky outcrop looking over
the lake and St Wolfgang, the Hotel Schafberg
awaits travellers.

Vineyard watchman in the southern Tyrol

A little further south, probably on the Merano side –
in this part of the Tyrol today Italian is spoken, but
in 1900 it was Austrian – the same affable spirit,
the same good life we can see at Ötz are evoked by
this picture. At the entrance to a vineyard, by an
arch decorated with an image of its saintly protector,
a watchman talks in a dignified manner with an
aproned vine-grower, while a little boy follows the
conversation attentively, holding on to the bundle
of grapes he has just collected. The watchman's
feathered felt hat, short loden coat, short leather
trousers drawn in at the knees and long unbleached
woollen socks – this would be the sort of outfit that
any child at the beginning of the twentieth century
would dream of.

Ötz, a village street

In the northern Tyrol, inhabitants of the village
of Ötz and its eponymous valley have lived for
centuries on the growing and weaving of linen.
Swiss, German and Italian merchants came for
supplies, and the region featured on the itineraries
of journeyman weavers completing their 'tour'
for their apprenticeships. But in the course of the
nineteenth century other visitors arrived in the
valley, brought by the railway. These first tourists
were less interested in the local linen trade than
the climate and the natural scenery: the Ötz Valley
is a magnificent region, surrounded by some of the
highest mountains in Austria and blessed with some
outstanding glaciers, gorges and waterfalls. Well
sheltered at the foot of the Acherkogel, Ötz benefits
from an exceptionally mild climate: fruit trees
flourish here, a local wine is made, and summer is
delightful. Today, the farmers of Ötz have left their
fields to devote themselves to their new customers,
and the village and its valley live on tourism, both in
summer and winter.

Panorama of Vienna *(preceding pages)*

'There is only one imperial city in the world, there is only Vienna' – so goes a popular song from the nineteenth century. The majestic capital of the Habsburgs was at that time the biggest and youngest of all European metropolises. Wagner compared it with Paris, calling it 'more beautiful and more gay', while nearly every nineteenth-century traveller commented on the good nature of the Viennese, the excellent food and wine, and the people's relaxed behaviour. On the most famous of Vienna's avenues, the Ring, is the Parliament (1883) and the Fountain of Minerva; further away, on the right, one can make out the Burgtheater (1888) opposite the town hall, the Rathaus (1883), whose high Gothic tower overlooks the Neoclassical Parliament building.

Innsbruck, Maria-Theresien-Strasse *(above)* and Herzog-Friedrich-Strasse *(opposite)*

In about 1000, some merchants settled on the left bank of the river Inn, in a position well suited for commerce between Germany and Italy. They erected a bridge and thus founded Innsbruck (literally 'bridge on the Inn'). At the beginning of the fifteenth century, Frederick I of Habsburg made Innsbruck his capital. His palace, the Hofburg, was to be rebuilt in 1766 by Maria Theresa, Empress of Austria, in the Baroque taste of the eighteenth century – as were the houses of Innsbruck's main street, Maria-Theresien-Strasse, whose façades, with their projecting bays and green slatted shutters, evoke both Italy and Bavaria. In this picture, just above the man pushing the handcart in the centre ground, is the Annasaüle, or Pillar of St Anne, a slender white column that stands out against the green of the mountainside. Erected in 1706, it commemorates the occasion when the inhabitants of Innsbruck chased the French and Bavarian enemies of the House of Austria out of their city in 1703. At the end of Maria-Theresien-Strasse is the start of Herzog-Friedrich-Strasse, where Frederick IV – 'the empty-pocketed', as his enemies ironically named him – had this delightful house (opposite) constructed at the beginning of the fifteenth century. It was restored in 1500 by Maximilian I, who added the projecting balcony decorated with polychrome figures and the famous golden roof of gilded copper tiles above.

Germany

Neuschwanstein Castle

Neuschwanstein, a dream in stone rising up out of nowhere,
a fantastical fortress perched on a rock and reaching for the skies:
this was the last castle of Ludwig II, King of Bavaria. A theatrical
set designer, Christian Jank, drew up the first plans for the castle,
which were revised and corrected by the king himself. From
the laying of the very first stone in 1869 until his tragic death in
1886, Ludwig II never once stopped intervening in the work of
the architects and designers who presided over the castle's
construction and the decoration of the interiors. So great yet so
contradictory were his desires for magnificence that, for Ludwig,
reality could never quite match up. The cost of this colossal
project emptied the kingdom's exchequers, which had already
been strained by the building of the palace at Herrenchiemsee.
Declared mad, Ludwig was imprisoned in Castle Berg, by the
shore of Lake Starnberg, where he drowned in mysterious
circumstances. Standing solitary on its rock, exposed to the
elements, Neuschwanstein (literally 'new rock of the swan')
remained unfinished. History, however, has done justice to the
last king of Bavaria: today, Neuschwanstein is the most visited
castle in Germany, and one of the most famous in Europe:
1.3 million tourists visit every year, 6,000 per day in summer.

The Rhine, the Lorelei rock

Before the advent of steamships there were only
fishing boats on the river's waves, and just below
the waterline at the foot of this black rock were
dangerous reefs. Sitting on the edge of the rock,
the blonde-haired Lorelei would comb her long hair
with a golden comb that shone in the sun, throwing
dazzling reflections onto the green waters of the
Rhine. The siren would sing. Captured by her
melody and blinded by the sparkling of the water,
the boats of the unfortunate fishermen would
be wrecked on the reefs, and the men would be
drowned. This is the legend that inspired Heinrich
Heine to write 'Die Lorelei', a Romantic poem that
German students learn to this day. Set to music at
the end of the 1830s, it became a world-famous
German song. The legend has a firm hold: even if
the nymph may have deserted her rock, her singing
may be heard every day as the tourist boats on the
Rhine pass by the dark domain of the Lorelei.

Limburg an der Lahn, the castle and the cathedral

What could be more bucolic than this view of
Limburg, slumbering by the banks of its river?
Once the residence of Eberhard, Count Palatine,
Limburg was founded in the tenth century by
Konrad Kurzbold, Graf von Niederlahngau, whose
sturdily built castle appears in front of St George's
Cathedral. The cathedral itself, with its seven
towers, was begun in 909 but not consecrated until
three centuries later, in 1235. A rare example of a
transitional style of architecture, it had recently been
restored by Limburg's Catholic bishopric when this
photochrome was taken.

Cologne Cathedral (overleaf)

The history of Cologne Cathedral is a serial in
several parts, informed by struggles between the
city's archbishops and inhabitants, and the
misadventures of history. On the 14 August 1248

Archbishop Konrad of Hochstaden laid the first
stone. One hundred and forty years later, in 1388,
the nave was opened for worship, and in 1447 the
bells were hung in the south tower. At the end
of the eighteenth century the occupying French
troops turned the cathedral into a market for animal
fodder and helped themselves to lead from the roof.
It was the kings of Prussia, Friedrich Wilhelm III
and Friedrich Wilhelm IV, who saved this imposing
masterpiece of Gothic architecture from total ruin.
Not without considerable expense, however –
according to some sources, the cost of reconstruction
(begun in 1842) ran to a total of 18,427,552 marks.
This sum was supplied through a combination
of state funds, private donations and money raised
by a lottery created specially for the purpose. At
last, on 15 October 1880, the cathedral's completion
was celebrated with great pomp and in the presence
of the Emperor Wilhelm I and almost all the
German princes.

An inhabitant of the Black Forest

With skirt and pinafore in black taffeta, white boots,
a blouse with big white puff sleeves, a broad-brimmed
straw hat tied under the chin and decorated with
roses in red wool (black would be worn by older
women), this young girl is wearing her Sunday
best. 'In the Black Forest, where all is life, vegetation,
rustling, perfume, pistil trembling, corolla open,
petal alive with colour, the country girl is dressed
like a flower', wrote Victor Hugo in 1840 in his travel
notebooks. Huddled around a bulbous bell tower,
the houses are 'just as the mountains have made
them . . . braving the rain beneath their big roofs
turned down over their eyes'.

Lindau, the entrance to the port

'What a delightful way of travelling it is to go by
river boat!' exclaimed the poet Théophile Gautier,
returning from a journey along the Rhine. And on
the lakes, no less: here, a boat slips slowly between
the lion and the lighthouse of the port of Lindau,
heading for the opposite bank of Lake Constance,
or for one of the pretty islands nearby covered
with vines, orchards, Romanesque churches
and monasteries.

Nuremberg

On Schütt Island, between two branches of the river
Pegnitz, a little group of people dance happily in a
circle on the riverbank. It is summer, the river flows
slowly past below the middle-class houses gathered
beside the dome of the Great Synagogue, and further
in the distance the spire of a bell tower points into
the pale sky where a few light clouds are floating.
The dawn of the twentieth century is rising over
Nuremberg. Visiting the city almost thirty years
later, in 1927, the writer Hermann Hesse felt deeply
uncomfortable: 'Nuremberg', he wrote, 'makes a
terrible impression on me. . . . The overarching
charm of the historic heart of the old city, with its
gracious fountain, all this beauty has been spoiled,
encased by a big city of business, without any
attraction, ugly, invaded by motor cars. . . . Everything
I see seems to me to be ready to collapse in just a few
hours' time, because there is neither any purpose
nor soul here.' Alas, Hesse saw it clearly: in a few
decades he was to be proved sadly right. In August
1938 the synagogue, built in 1874, was demolished

on the orders of the Nazi party – a symbolic act
of destruction, intended to 'serve as an example'.
It was dramatic prelude to the bloody episodes of
the Second World War, in which of the rest of the
city would be severely damaged.

Munich, the Hofbrauhaus (opposite)

According to a guidebook from the 1950s, 'even
if many Munich intellectuals make a face when
strangers who have barely set foot in the city start
by asking the way to the Hofbrauhaus, it is a good
idea to begin a tour of Munich by visiting the famous
brewery, since it is there that one will gain the most
penetrating insight, so to speak, into the soul of
the city.' Other famous sights include the Residenz
and the Asamkirche (the church of St Johann
Nepomuk), a Baroque jewel where the eye roves
around in disbelief, looking in vain for some little
patch of unadorned emptiness.

Hildesheim (overleaf, left)

In the land of the Tales of the Brothers Grimm,
in the shadow of the dark forested hills of the Harz
range, ancient medieval cities such as Goslar and
Hildesheim stand as testament to the rich history
of this commercial region. 'Hildesheim was a
dream, a dream in broad daylight that has lasted
a thousand years', wrote the German author and
translator Hans-Egon Gerlach, sadly evoking the
terrible bombardments that destroyed the city
in 1945. There were hundreds of half-timbered
houses in Hildesheim like those shown here,
lining a branch of the river Innerste. There used to
be little streets, fountains, squares and fourteen
churches. Three of them have survived; and
alongside of the Chapel of the Virginan old rose
bush flowers every year.

The Drachenschlucht Gorge, near Eisenach (overleaf, right)

Medieval Thuringia, with its fortified castles and
singing contests, had its seat at Wartburg, a
formidable fortress built above Eisenach in the heart
of the forest. On the route to Wartburg Castle, the
Drachenschlucht Gorge – well known to hikers –
makes an impressively chaotic impression. At the
beginning of spring a torrent runs through these
rocks, making a grinding sound that evokes the noise
of the dragon that is said to roam this wild place.

Berlin, Café Bauer on Unter den Linden

Berlin was a centre of frenetic activity during
the Belle Epoque, teeming with non-stop traffic,
bicycles, omnibuses and trams, all cluttering the
streets and filling them with the sounds of engines
and horns. On his return from Germany in 1892,
Mark Twain published an article on Berlin in the
New York Sun, under the title 'The German Chicago',
in which he praised Berliners' pragmatism and
competence. But in Berlin itself, the intelligentsia
was becoming concerned about this 'American-style'
materialism that threatened humanist values.
At the Romanische Café on the Kurfürstendamm
artists, writers and opponents of the regime met
and debated fiercely. But at the Café Bauer, at the
corner of Friedrichstrasse and Unter den Linden,
the clientele was more mixed, the atmosphere less
filled with anxiety. Here, one could unwind amid the
Roman-style frescoes by Anton von Werner, drink
Turkish or Viennese coffee, nibble on some of the
pastries and leaf through one of the six hundred

newspapers on offer at one's leisure. Completely in
the spirit of its age, the Café Bauer (given one star
by the Baedeker guide) was the place to be seen.

Berlin, the cathedral and the Friedrichsbrücke

Since 1890, the capital of the German empire under Wilhelm II had been expanding at a great rate. The emperor – militarist, stubborn and badly advised – dreamed of glory and wanted to assert his power in every domain. Berlin beat to the rhythm of concerts and military parades, imposing buildings rose from the ground on every street corner, and old monuments judged 'too monarchical' were systematically demolished to be replaced by others more symbolic, more worthy of the new German power. Columns, memorials and a triumphal arch were all raised to impress the Emperor Franz Joseph of Austria when he visited Berlin. Wilhelm himself did not like the city's Baroque cathedral, already rebuilt by Karl Friedrich Schinkel in 1820–22, which he found antiquated and poorly adapted to its age – that is to say, 'too monarchical'. He had it demolished and commissioned the architect Julius Raschdorff to build a new one in the style of the

Italian Renaissance, and to make it very tall, so that it dominated all Berlin. Between 1894 and 1905 the building was slowly constructed, provoking much discussion: the optimists (supporters of the emperor) were satisfied, while the pessimists (the liberals) mocked the slow progress of the building work. Berliners developed the habit of taking their Sunday walks by the Friedrichsbrücke (Frederick's Bridge) in order to have a look at the building site. The new cathedral was finished in 1905, so this photochrome can be dated to that year, or soon after.

Potsdam, the Windmill (opposite)

There were at one time three windmills in Potsdam: the one that survives is a recent replica of a mill dating back to 1790. The oldest was constructed in 1747 – the year in which Frederick the Great's Summer Palace was finished – and is associated with a legend concerning the king's character. It was said that Frederick, disturbed by the noise it made, offered to buy the mill from its owner. The miller refused. Piqued, Frederick is said to have exclaimed, 'Doesn't he know that I have the power to seize his windmill without giving him a single penny?', to which the miller is supposed to have replied, 'Certainly Your Majesty, Your Majesty may be able to do that, but with all due respect to Your Majesty, the Court of Appeal in Berlin is there to be used!' The king became so fond of 'his' windmill that he made great efforts to replace it when it fell into disrepair. In 1790 Frederick paid the architect Cornelius Wilhelm van der Bosch out of his own pocket to build a large mill of the Dutch type on the same spot. It was burnt to a cinder on 27 April 1945, when a Soviet tank attacked from the palace entrance.

Dresden, view of the old city

In the foreground, the Elbe, wide and peaceful, smooth as a mirror; above, the Saxony sky, delicately coloured, serene; between the two, a magnificent city: Dresden, the 'Florence of the Elbe', as the eighteenth-century poet and philosopher Johann Gottfried Herder baptized it. The Neoclassical pitched roof right of centre belongs to the Opera House, where works by the greatest composers were performed and which for a period was closely associated with Richard Wagner. His operas *Rienzi*, *Der Fliegende Holländer* ('The Flying Dutchman') and *Tannhaüser* were all performed here during the 1840s, while he worked as court conductor. By 1849, however, the composer's revolutionary politics obliged him to leave Dresden.

Hamburg, the new sailing port, Asia Quay

The third biggest in Europe, the port of Hamburg
at the end of the nineteenth century stretched over
6 kilometres (3¹⁄₄ miles) from Altona to the Bille
dike. In 1902 J.-K. Huysmans described it as follows:
'Everywhere, on every side, there are brickwork
docks . . . grimy from the sea spray, blackened by
the smoke from machines, run through with rails,
with goods trains that stretch as far as the eye can
see. . . . The warehouses and halls follow your steps
endlessly, and one ends up by thinking that one
will never see the end of them; you can probe the
horizon, and it reveals itself to be planted with a
forest of masts, tall plantations of steamers' funnels,
bristling with dock cranes rummaging in the bellies
of ships. . . . One senses an immense, silent effort:
this relentless labour is carried out without a sound;
it is only seldom, at rare intervals, that one can hear
the horns of the ships as they make their way to the
open sea.'

Hamburg, the Steckelhörnfleet

In Hamburg's old city, barges would pass from the
northern port on the Elbe to the docks in the lower
Alster basin along the narrow Steckelhörn canal.
Its deep water, lined with old Hanseatic residential
buildings, leads to a branch of the river Alster that
winds around the Nikolaikirche. This Lutheran
church, whose high carved tower can be seen in the
background, was built to the designs of the English
architect Sir George Gilbert Scott after the great
fire that ravaged the city in 1842. On the square in
front of the church was the Hopfenmarkt, once 'the
liveliest market in Hamburg' (according to the 1888
Baedeker guide). In common with most of the city's
churches, the Nikolaikirche was mostly destroyed by
bombing in 1943; it was never rebuilt, but beyond its
ruins a memorial was erected.

Heligoland

The coat of arms of Heligoland include the colours green (for the earth), red (for the cliffs) and white (for the sand). This little triangular island is in the North Sea, some 100 kilometres (60 miles) from the mouth of the Elbe in Schleswig-Holstein. One arrives on Heligoland on the southern shore, but the village itself is perched on the Oberland (Upper Land), a verdant plateau 63 metres (200 feet) above sea level. You may of course go up on foot using the stairs, but there is also a lift that was built in the 1870s. The poet Heinrich Heine spent the summer of 1825 on Heligoland, when the island was under English control. When Franz Kafka stayed here in 1903 Heligoland was Prussian: Wilhelm II had exchanged it in 1890 for the colony of Zanzibar.

Norderney, the beach

Along the coast of East Frisia, between the Ems and the Weser, is a flat stretch of country with half-barren expanses, where clumps of juniper grow here and there – a melancholy landscape where the acrid smell of peat bogs mixes with the cold, salty sea wind. The invigorating air here has always appealed to visitors in search of a healthy retreat and some bathing. Every summer since the end of the nineteenth century, German and Danish tourists have frequented the beaches and islands of the North Sea. Arriving from Bremerhaven, four or five hours away, or from Norden, less than one hour away, they landed on the East Frisian islands: Juist, Baltrum and Norderney. In the 1890s Norderney was one of the most popular places for bathing in Germany, attracting some 12,000 visitors. With its typical wicker beach-chairs, the beach (known as the Strand) was a meeting place for strangers, although the Baedeker guide reminds us that 'men's and women's bathing are separate until 2 o'clock'.

Denmark

Copenhagen, the Stock Exchange

With its wide roads lined with tall buildings, the capital of
Denmark immediately gave nineteenth-century visitors the
impression that they were entering a big city – even more so
if they had just arrived by train or by steamship, crossing the
peaceful countryside of Zealand on the way, with its many
windmills. The Copenhagen Stock Exchange, built during the
reign of Christian IV (1588–1648), is dominated by an ornate spire
decorated with four gold and green dragons with interlaced tails.

Copenhagen, Vor Frelsers Kirke

The most recognizable feature of the Vor Frelsers
Kirke (the Church of Our Saviour) is its spire,
around which winds a curious staircase with a
high balustrade. French author Xavier Marmier,
a promoter of Scandinavian literature who travelled
all over Denmark, Sweden and Norway in the 1830s,
saw this stairway as a mystical symbol representing
humankind's thoughts climbing to heaven.

Copenhagen, the entrance to
the Tivoli Gardens

The entrance to the Tivoli Gardens – a name adopted
by many public parks in the bigger cities of Europe –
is situated directly opposite the railway station, so
that new arrivals cannot ignore its existence. In the
middle of the gardens are theatres, a music hall and
some excellent restaurants. Open-air balls, firework
displays and illuminations made the Tivoli Gardens
a popular destination for families. The Danes,
despite their somewhat austere reputation, would
stay there beyond midnight.

Norway

Bergen, the fish market

The sharp light of the northern Atlantic bathes this view of
Bergen. A port on the west coast of Norway, Bergen has been a
gateway to Southern Europe since the Middle Ages. There fish
are sold by the boatload or live, in tanks. The trade in cod and
haddock, some weighing up to 70 kilograms (150 pounds),
constituted the inhabitants' principal resource at the beginning of
the twentieth century. The market was evidently very picturesque:
around 1870 one visitor (Paul du Chaillu, a Franco-American
explorer) could see 'a mother and her son carrying an enormous
cod between them', and 'a solid-looking man buckling under the
weight of a fish that was bigger than he was'.

Opheim, the Hotel Froemnes

In the rosy light of sunset – or more likely the first
glows of red announcing the arrival of spring after
a long Norwegian winter – a hotel perches on an
inlet of the Hardanger fjord. Situated on a green
strip of land that juts out into the calm waters of the
lake, with dark pine forest and twinkling glaciers
rising behind it, during the high season the hotel
welcomed tourists, travellers and lovers of nature.

The midnight sun near Hammerfest

Just before you reach the North Cape, Hammerfest
in the bay of Fuglenes is the last important port in
Finnmark, the northern- and easternmost county
of Norway. From the beginning of May until the end
of July, night never falls. Instead the sun stays on the
horizon, from which it begins to rise at midnight,
lighting up the sea and giving the Sorø mountains
an intense blue colour. It is a spectacle that can be
admired to the full from the summit of Tyvefield,
which dominates the town.

Family of Lapps in front of their settlement (above); Lapps and reindeer (opposite)

A nomadic people from the far north of Europe, the Sami are great reindeer breeders who were displaced into territory extending into four countries: Norway, Sweden, Finland and Russia. Colonized, forced to convert to Christianity and renamed 'Lapps' (which means 'ragged' in Finno-Ugric), the Sami tribe were even banned from using their own language until as late as the 1960s. The Sami used to live in tents of coarse canvas, covered with thatch or reindeer skins and held up by four long poles. A hole in the centre of the canvas allowed the smoke to escape from the fire that heated the tent during the day. Today, around 10 to 15 per cent of Samis still breed reindeer – on a very large scale – and practise transhumance, taking animals to graze on new pastures, often over long distances. Indefatigable

draft animals, reindeer may be ridden bareback or fitted with a saddle made from reindeer skin called the *pulkka*. They can travel for 50 kilometres (30 miles) a day without becoming tired. When a family were moving on, they would load their baggage and their children onto the backs of five or six reindeer, which would be attached to each other, and the family would walk at the head of the convoy, with the father leading the first animal.

*The Kjendal Glacier seen from Loen
(overleaf)*

Further north than the Sogn Fjord, the Nordfjord
penetrates far into the mainland. At its extreme
east, the village of Loen benefits from a unique
view of one of the biggest glaciers in Norway,
the Kjendal Glacier. Perched on a rock, a solitary
traveller contemplates the bluish chaos of this
frozen desert of ice.

The whaler Duncan Grey *at Skaarø*

All along the coast of Finnmark from the North Cape
to the Barents Sea, whaling used to be practised –
as here at Skaarø, an island in the Atlantic north
of Tromsø. Different species of whale were hunted,
whose numbers varied year by year. The geographer-
explorer Charles Rabot reported in 1885 that 'one is
invited to shoot a whale as one might be invited to
shoot a pheasant in our country.' At the end of the
nineteenth century whalers were small steamboats,
solidly built, fast and fitted with a cannon on a
mobile platform at the front. A harpoon with an
explosive shell at the sharpened point would be shot
from the barrel of the cannon; it would be attached
by a retractable cable to the hold of the boat.
'Four steel teeth . . . at the moment of explosion,
open like the struts of an umbrella and dig deep into
the animal's flesh.' The sea would be marbled with

pools of blood, and the harpooned beast would
struggle desperately, dragging the boat along in its
path and beating the surface of the water with its tail.
These days only fishing for Minke whales continues
in Norway, and fortunately hunting on an industrial
scale has disappeared.

Large and small whales on the shore at Skaarø

Once the whale had been brought to the shore, the cutting and carving up began. For that, the whalers would use knives about a metre long and as sharp as razors. A man would have to get inside the whale (he would disappear completely) and force his way through the carcass to reach the internal organs. There would be a suffocating smell when the organs spilled out onto the shore. In this picture the carnage has not yet begun; the photographer must have left before the proceedings were over.

Spitsbergen, view of Smeerenburg

In the seventeenth and eighteenth centuries, a time
of epic whaling expeditions, Spitsbergen (the largest
island in the Svalbard archipelago) was occupied
in turn by the French, the Dutch and the English.
In the nineteenth and twentieth centuries it became
a destination for scientific expeditions – peaceful
ones, at last. Meteorological and astronomical
field trips and studies of glaciers, flora and fauna
followed one after the other. At the north-west of
the archipelago, on the island of Amsterdam,
Smeerenburg was used as a base by Dutch whalers
between 1620 and 1660. All that remains today are
the traces of a few ovens in which the whale blubber
was heated to extract oil.

Spitsbergen, Andrée's scientific station at Danskøya

On 11 July 1897, after twenty years of research, the Swedish engineer and aeronautical scientist Salomon August Andrée launched himself from the island of Danskøya in a hydrogen balloon in an attempt to reach the geographic North Pole. He was joined by two other team members: the engineer Knut Frænkel and the photographer Nils Strindberg. It is these three men we see in this extremely rare document, which shows Professor Andrée's base and his balloon, 'the Eagle', shortly before launching. The balloon rose into the air and remained visible for an hour as it headed north, until it was no more than a tiny dot against the grey sky. Then it disappeared, for ever. In August 1930 a Norwegian team made a macabre discovery on White Island, where the three aeronauts had met their deaths. The skeletons of Andrée and his companions were identified thanks to the vessel's log, which was found intact, carefully wrapped in oiled straw, next to Andrée's mortal remains.

Sweden

Stockholm seen from the island of Riddarholmen

'Imagine a large city . . . crossed by canals and dotted with gardens laid out with groups of trees, set on seven islands like Rome on its seven hills.' Here is Stockholm, set between the Baltic Sea and Lake Mälaren, and called both the 'Venice of the North' and the 'city between the bridges'. The Swedish author Selma Lagerlöf has also been given it the poetic title 'the village that swims on the water'. At the turn of the nineteenth century people would travel around on little steamboats.

Stockholm, the Katarina Lift

Since 1883, the Katarina Lift (Katarinahissen) has
stood out against the Stockholm sky like an Eiffel
Tower – or, more precisely, the new Katarina Lift,
which was reconstructed in the 1930s, but which
continues to carry visitors up to the Södermalm
district, where they can admire the magnificent
panorama of the city laid out before them. But the
Katarina Lift was not built solely for the purposes
of amusement: it also allowed inhabitants to avoid
making a wide detour to reach the old districts
perched on the cliff.

Gothenburg Horticultural Society

'I would like to be able to tell of a storm, but
unfortunately the weather was very fine': so reported
a nineteenth-century traveller, somewhat regretfully,
on his way to Gothenburg on the western coast of
Sweden. The most important port in Sweden and
the only one with access to the sea on the western
coast, Gothenburg was a prosperous city, a rival for
Stockholm, where well-off merchants could live
comfortably. They would frequent the Horticultural
Society's gardens (created in 1842), which boasted
a music pavilion and a Palm House typical of
glasshouses based the famous example at Kew
Gardens, London.

Finland

The Imatra Rapids

A country of lakes, rivers, waterfalls and immense forests of pine, fir and birch trees, Finland is a vast maze of land and water illuminated by the incomparable northern light. In the Gulf of Finland, Karelia – where Imatra is situated – is a province that stands for Finnish identity. Powerfully dominated by the Russian empire, the biggest part of its territory was also annexed by the Soviet Union at the end of the Second World War. Not far from the border with Russia but today firmly Finnish, Imatra was a well known holiday destination in 1900, frequented by rich tourists from St Petersburg. At the Imatra Falls – the 'local Niagara' – a hotel with electricity awaited them.

Poland

Warsaw, Krakow Avenue

In Warsaw, at one end of Krakow Avenue – today Krakowskie
Street – is the Castle Square. The former palace of Sigismund
the Old was enlarged by Sigismund III Vasa, who moved his
court here in 1596 when Warsaw replaced Krakow as the capital
of Poland. The column to Sigismund III, sculpted by Clemente
Molli, was raised opposite the castle tower in 1644 by King
Wladislaw IV in memory of his father. Subject to occupation –
by Sweden, Russia, Prussia, Austria, France, then Russia again
(at the time this image was taken, in 1890), and Germany –
Warsaw has always had to reassert its autonomy. It was
between 1764 and 1795, under the reign of Stanislas II, the last
independent king of Poland, that Warsaw experienced its most
enlightened artistic period. A great admirer of Italian painting,
the king invited the artist Bernardo Bellotto to his court, who
painted twenty-six panoramas of Warsaw and Wilanow. Bellotto's
works were used for reference by the architects who rebuilt
Warsaw after the Second World War.

Danzig, view of the Krahntor

At the confluence of the Mottlau and the Vistula,
Danzig (modern Gdansk) was the capital of
eastern Prussia, and in 1890 one of the principal
commercial ports on the Baltic coast. At the
beginning of the fourteenth century it was a fortified
Hanseatic city, but during the following centuries
it was besieged many times. Danzig eventually
became an autonomous city of Poland and remained
Polish until 1793, when it was occupied by Prussia,
then taken by Napoleon's armies, and returned to
Prussia in 1814. The typical architecture of this lovely
trade city is that of the time of the Hanseatic League:
gabled houses and old grain lofts, as in Hamburg
or Lübeck. On the Mottlau quay, opposite the docks,
the Krahntor housed two mills. Polish once more
in 1945, Gdansk was carefully rebuilt and restored.
The sixth-biggest city in Poland, Gdansk is also the
country's biggest port.

Breslau, the town hall

In the south-west of Poland, not far from the
Czech border, Breslau – today known as Wroclaw –
has always been the meeting point of various
cultural influences: Slav, Bohemian, Polish,
Austrian, German . . . On the Market Square, the
sixteenth-century town hall, a harmonious blend
of German Late Gothic and Nordic architecture,
is a magnificent illustration of this cultural mix.
The tower is decorated with a Renaissance lantern and
today houses the Museum of the History of Wroclaw.
In front of the main part of the building, which dates
from 1270 and was used for many years as a market
hall, stands the statue of Aleksander Count Fredro,
the 'Polish Molière'. This satirical playwright also
served in the Polish wing of Napoleon's armies.
He never received proper recognition until after his
death in 1896 – another thing he had in common
with Molière.

Latvia

Riga, the railway bridge

Built in the thirteenth century on an island in the Daugava River, not far from where it flows out into the Baltic Sea, Riga was always a transit city and a very important port – originally it was at the heart of the Hanseatic League (in the hands of the German church), and then became Polish, Swedish and Russian in turn. Since east and west have always met here, the Latvian capital, surrounded by its fortified enclosure, suffer numerous assaults by its neighbours. In addition, the Daugava River (the 'river of destiny'), upon which the city depended, frequently flooded with catastrophic results. Between 1701 and 1888 a series of different bridges was built, on floating pontoons, that were assembled in spring and taken down again on 1 November; and in the 1860s, when the railway arrived, a railway bridge became a necessity. This iron structure, built between 1871 and 1873, was used by trains, pedestrians and wagons. To cross, one had to pay a levy: it cost 5 kopecks for a hand cart, 6 kopecks for an empty cart drawn by a horse and 10 kopecks for a full cart. Pedestrians, doctors' carriages, firemen, priests and police were all exempt from the charge. Beneath the bridge, in the foreground of this picture, large rafts of logs floated down the Daugava towards the Baltic, where the cargo ships were waiting.

Russia

Moscow, St Basil's Cathedral

On 1 October 1552, on the Orthodox feast day of the Intercession of the Virgin, Ivan the Terrible seized the city of Kazan from the Tartars, a victory predicted by Basil the Fortunate, one of those mad simpletons with visionary gifts who are often to be found in Russian popular tradition and literature. To commemorate this event and to give thanks to heaven, the Blessed Virgin and the holy man, the Tsar ordered the architect Postnik Yakovlev to design a basilica that would surpass in beauty every religious edifice that had ever been built. Postnik created an exuberant cathedral on the ground plan of a Greek cross, following the model of Hagia Sophia in Constantinople. The great tower in the centre, surrounded by smaller towers and topped by a gilded dome, was 57 metres (190 feet) high; and four large onion domes – each accompanied by smaller domes and surmounted by golden crosses – marked the cardinal points. An extraordinary oriental confection in bright colours, like a crown set in the centre of Red Square, St Basil's was finished in 1561. It is claimed that the Tsar had his architect's eyes put out so that he could never reproduce anything so beautiful again.

Arkhangelsk, a shipment of cod

At the mouth of the Northern Dvina on the White
Sea, Arkhangelsk (formerly known in English as
Archangel) was a prosperous town in the Middle
Ages, and Russia's first port. Merchants came from
all over Europe to buy fish, wood and furs, notably
the English, who benefitted from commercial
agreements they had drawn up in the sixteenth
century with Tsar Ivan the Terrible. In 1693
Peter I ordered the construction of a naval base at
Arkhangelsk, had the town fortified, and carried
out his victorious military operations against
the Swedes from here. The port suffered from a
severe handicap, however: it was closed in by ice
for five months of the year, during which time the
fleet was stuck. This considerable inconvenience
obliged Peter to leave the town in 1703 in favour of
St Petersburg, his new capital. At first Arkhangelsk
went into decline, but the White Sea port recovered
thanks to fishing. In 1818 the writer Bernardin de
Saint-Pierre reported that 'From the ice of this ocean,
every year a prodigious multitude of herrings comes
forth'. One hundred years later, a photochrome of
the Dvina quayside shows tons of salted cod being
unloaded from a boat – an activity that continues to
this day.

Country girl from Arkhangelsk

With her heavy damask skirt, white blouse with
big sleeves, camisole and headdress richly decorated
with red embroidery, this woman is wearing
clothes for a feast day. The colour red traditionally
symbolizes life and the sun.

Frozen tundra, district of Arkhangelsk
(overleaf)

Here in the midnight sun are Samoyedic people
travelling by reindeer – 'sweet creatures that look so
fragile, with their fine legs and antlers', as Théophile
Gautier once described them.

St Petersburg, the Beloselsky-Belozersky Palace and Anichkov Bridge

Far from the heart of Russia, reclaimed by super-human efforts from the marshes by order of Peter the Great, St Petersburg has inspired varied and contradictory reflections by writers and travellers of centuries past. Great enthusiasm has been expressed for the 'strange' beauty of the Nevsky Prospekt; for the Bronze Horseman (the statue of Peter the Great); for the granite quays decorated with magnificent parapets; the plasterwork of the city's façades, in ochre, red, pink and green; and for its 'six months of white ground'. Great criticism has been voiced, too: it has been called city of millionaires where only princes and generals are to be seen, a town where foreign languages are never heard, with gigantic edifices in bad taste and squares that are simply too vast, streets that are too straight. . . . The streets of St Petersburg have particularly fascinated travellers, who could talk on the topic for ever. They are in fact remade every year, since they are so badly damaged by the thaw. Even when the rough stones were superseded by granite paving slabs in the nineteenth century, it was still necessary to replace many of them at the end of the winter. That is what the workmen are doing in this picture, on the Anichkov Bridge, while light horse-drawn carriages trot across.

St Petersburg, the Neva and the quayside for the imperial yachts

'Between the milky water and the pearly sky . . . the magnificent outline of St Petersburg, whose amethyst shades divide these two pale immensities with a line of demarcation . . . nothing was more splendid than this golden city . . . where the evening was as pale as the dawn' (Théophile Gautier, 1858). On the Neva, where some sheets of ice are still floating, the Tsar's yachts are moored in front of the Neoclassical façade of the palace of Count Nikolai Petrovich Rumiantsev, constructed in 1824. On the right can be seen the yacht *Alexandria*, built in 1851 for Nicholas I and named after his wife, Alexandra Fedorovna. The *Alexandria* was used by every sovereign of Russia for fifty years. Tsar Nicholas II, for instance, welcomed the German emperor Wilhelm II and the French president Félix Faure on board.

Moscow, the Kremlin (overleaf)

A panorama of Moscow, through which the Moskva river winds sinuously, tracing a semicircle in front of the Kremlin. This unusual view was taken from the crenellated fortifications of the Kremlin, and includes the Borovitskaya Tower. At the centre of the picture are the gilded onion domes of the Cathedral of Christ the Redeemer.

Moscow, the Iberian Gate

This picture shows one of the entrances to Red
Square, the Iberian (or Resurrection) Gate, 'which
is the object of such veneration . . . that no one may
enter with their head covered, even aristocrats', as
Théophile Gautier remarked with surprise. Between
the gate's two arches is the small Chapel of the
Holy Virgin of Iberia, in front of which Muscovites,
including the Tsar, always took off their hats, even if
'it is not pleasant to hold one's fur hat in one's hand
when the temperature is twenty-five degrees below
zero'. The chapel contains a copy of a miraculous
icon housed in the Iberian (or Iveron) Monastery
on Mount Athos, Greece, which is said to have bled
after an attack. The gate was completely dismantled
in the Soviet period because it hindered tanks from
parading in Red Square, but it was reopened in 1996
and the chapel reconsecrated.

Moscow, Tsar Kolokol (the Tsar of Bells)

There are so many stories relating to this bell that
it is difficult to tell the true from the false. When
was it founded? Some say in 1725; according to
others, it was cast in 1733, or 1735, or even in 1737.
Moreover, some people maintain that fragments
of an earlier bell – made in the sixteenth century
but destroyed by fire in 1701 – were made up into
the Tsar Kolokol, but that it cracked at the time
of casting. As for Tsar Kolokol's size and weight,
sources are more or less in agreement: the bell
weighs approximately 200 tonnes, with a height
and diameter of about 6 metres (20 feet). The
fragment that can be seen at the foot of the plinth
weighs about 11 tonnes. Most historians maintain
that the bell in fact cracked through thermic shock
during the water stage of founding; and most
people agree that it will never ring.

Russia 153

A Russian beggar

These eyes belong to a man who has been aged by privation, who is worn out and empty-handed but still standing. He is one of those poor people whose cruel fate was scarcely improved by the abolition of serfdom in 1861: the peasants were now free, but they were also without means, and remained subject to the goodwill of land owners. Frequently they were conscripted by force into the army or were reduced to begging and exile. Whole villages fell empty as their populations wandered in search of food. Maxim Gorky knew this misery: Nizhny Novgorod was his native town, and as an orphan he had been left to fend for himself from the age of ten, unloading ships on the river.

Nizhny Novgorod

At first sight Venice comes to mind. But this is not Venice, nor is it the sea: it is Nizhny Novgorod, a great trade centre whose vast territory is spread across the confluence of the Oka and the Volga. The villages on the outskirts have kept traces of their old fortifications, built during the time of the Tartar and Mongol invasions in the fourteenth century. It was around the beginning of the nineteenth century, under the domination of the princes of Moscow, that Nizhny and its satellite boroughs were developed. In 1817, the fair celebrated by the neighbouring monastery of Makaryev was moved onto the opposite bank of the Oka, which was linked to Nizhny by a bridge of boats. 'The crowds were overflowing there', wrote Théophile Gautier. 'On both sides, the river disappeared beneath a huge swarming mass of boats. . . . Perched up on the high saddles of their little horses, Cossacks in charge of policing the fair rode up and town with serious expressions . . . through the *drozhkis*, the *telegas*, carriages of every kind and passers-by of both sexes.' Gautier went on to describe tea houses where business was conducted, the encampments of Siberian fur merchants and ships carrying huge quantities of grain.

Caucasus, the Vladikavkas region

Riding near the foothills of the Caucasus Mountains
– the great range that can be seen here, turning pink
in the setting sun – these horsemen are Cossacks,
whose fathers put them on horseback at the age of
six or seven years old. Vladikavkaz is the capital of
North Ossetia, which is located in the southern part
of the Caucasus on the borders with Turkey and
Persia, and close to Georgia, which explains the
presence of Persians, Russians and Ottomans. The
population of the Vladikavkas region was therefore
very mixed: Caucasians, Armenians, Georgians,
Russians, Orthodox Christians, Jews, Shi'ite and
Sunni Muslims, and even Hindus – all became
established here from the fifth century onwards.
In the eighteenth and nineteenth centuries
Vladikavkaz traded with Tbilisi, its Georgian
neighbour, to which it was linked by a main road

in 1799. In the caravanserai of Tbilisi, the Ossetian
merchants traded their furs and woollens for
Persian silk. The annexation of Georgia by Russia
in 1801, the wars waged here by European countries,
rebellions against various invaders and, in our own
times, Chechen separatism have made the Caucasus
a region with a tragic destiny.

Caucasus, Tartar house

The Tartars originally lived under the nomadic Turkic khanate of the north of China. In the thirteenth century, chased westwards by the Mongols, the Tartars from the khanate of Batu – the grandson of Genghis Khan – established themselves between the Volga and the river Kama, where they prospered. Until the nineteenth century, that is, when their territories were pillaged by Russian landowners who had been dispossessed of their serfs, and when they began to seek out their country of origin again. At the beginning of the twentieth century the Tartars of the Caucasus grouped together in the same districts and lived in wooden houses with outside galleried areas, while in the countryside many retained a nomadic way of life, living in tents. Here, the head of the family is dressed in a long kaftan and a traditional fur headdress. Behind him, the women are wearing traditional costume, decorated with coloured embroidery, and headscarves (the Tartars are Muslims).

Ukraine

Kiev, the banks of the Dnieper

Founded in the ninth century by Slavs and Varangians from Scandinavia, the Ukraine (formerly the Kievan Rus) was the first Slav state, and Kiev, its capital, is considered the 'mother of all Russian cities'. Between the Dnieper and the Black Sea, every spring the boatmen would bring their cargoes towards Constantinople, where they would trade for gold and silk. Constantinople's Byzantine splendour convinced the young prince of Kiev, Vladimir, to convert to Christianity. His baptism – and that of all his subjects – in the Dnieper in 988 marked the beginning of a great wave of evangelization. The oldest monastery in Russia, the Pechersk Lavra, is in Kiev: in its catacombs, the *pechery* (literally 'caves'), the relics of three hundred saints lie at rest. In the nineteenth century countless faithful pilgrims from all over Russia came to visit the monastery. This photochrome evokes a passage by Nikolai Gogol, born in the Ukraine in 1809: 'How beautiful the Dnieper is, when in calm weather its waves roll freely through forests and hills! . . . You would think it was made of glass – it seems as though this were a blue road, like a mirror, immensely wide, infinitely long, swirling and rushing forward. . . . How beautiful it is, the Dnieper, on a hot summer's night, when all is sleeping, man, beast and bird; God alone in his majesty contemplates the sky and the earth, and shakes his clothes with dignity. The stars burst forth; they burn and light up the world and every one of them is reflected in the Dnieper.'

Odessa, the Potemkin Steps

Odessa and the Crimea have always stood out
from the rest of the Ukraine. Conquered in 1794
by Grigory Potemkin, Catherine II's great love, the
Crimea and Odessa began to welcome the empire's
'undesirable subjects', notably Jews set free by
Catherine who came to trade there. In the nineteenth
century all of Europe took an interest in the Crimea.
Odessa was administered by a French nobleman
exiled during the Revolution – Armand Duplessis,
duc de Richelieu, whose statue may be seen at the
top of the famous steps, which rise to a height of
142 metres (465 feet) and were formerly names
after him. Pushkin, exiled to Odessa in 1823, wrote
that 'In Odessa one can smell Europe!' Odessa,
a cosmopolitan city, is Russia's first port and naval
base on the Black Sea. It was here in 1905 that the
Potemkin uprising took place: the battleship's sailors,
who had rebelled against their oppressive officers,
joined striking workers to demonstrate. Some
sources say that the crowd fired by dismounted
cavalry at the Steps. During the Second World War
the population of Odessa, starved by the Soviet
government, was deported en masse under the
control of the Red Army.

Alupka, the Vorontsov Palace

This thousand-and-one-nights palace is the
former residence of Count (later Prince) Mikhail
Semyonovich Vorontsov, a brilliant officer who
distinguished himself at the time of the Napoleonic
Wars. Appointed Governor-General of the Crimea in
1823, he established his residence on the Black Sea
at Alupka. Raised in England, Vorontsov entrusted
the design of his palace to Edward Blore, worked on
Buckingham Palace and on alterations to St James's
Palace. Built between 1826 and 1846, the palace at
Alupka combines Moorish, Tudor and neo-Gothic
styles. On the southern façade, a fresco bears the
inscription in Arabic 'There is no conqueror but
Allah.' The immense park includes a botanic garden
created by the German master gardener and botanist
Carolus Antonius Keebach.

Czech Republic

Karlsbad, the New Spring

'To be comfortable in Karlsbad', noted Baron Pollnitz in his *Memoirs*, 'one must bring three things: a bed, some wine and a cook.' But the Baron was a man of the eighteenth century and he was speaking of Karlsbad (present-day Karlovy Vary) in 1740, in an era when the oldest thermal spa town in Bohemia was still 'a spring – a relatively gentle one – where one may grow thoroughly bored'. The resort was transformed at the end of the eighteenth century and still more so in the nineteenth, adapting itself to meet the tastes of modern spa enthusiasts. The buildings were extended and modernized, and new ones were built, such as the Neue Sprudel (the 'New Spring'), attributed to the Viennese architects Ferdinand Feller and Hermann Helmer. A colonnade in wrought iron and cast iron, finished in 1880, ran the length of the establishment and enclosed the fountain. The staff were highly qualified and included doctors who spoke several languages – the clientele was mostly foreign, coming from Russia, Germany, Austria, France and England. At the dawn of the twentieth century Karlsbad was visited for its society life as much as for its waters: 134 families visited Karlsbad in 1756, whereas between 1890 and 1911 the number of spa enthusiasts rose from 26,000 to 71,000.

Prague, Charles Bridge

Prague, at the heart of old Bohemia, features
memorably in Michel Tournier's book *Lieux dits*.
He describes the meeting that took place at the Café
Alcron on Sunday 26 January 1786 between Mozart,
his librettist Lorenzo da Ponte and Casanova, newly
escaped from his imprisonment in Venice. Mozart's
opera *Don Giovanni*, loosely based on Casanova's
amatory exploits, received its premiere in Prague
the following year. In the 'picture-postcard Prague'
of the Belle Epoque, this particular photochrome
picture shows the façades of the old town stretched
out along the banks of the Moldau (Vltava), on either
side of the entrance tower to the Charles Bridge. The
bridge itself, built in 1357 under the reign of Charles
IV, was for a long time the only bridge in the city.

Prague, the Tyn church

The most beautiful Gothic church in Prague, Our
Lady before Tyn (Tynsky Chram), has dominated
the Old Town Square since the fourteenth century.
Its construction, which lasted one hundred and fifty
years, was financed by German merchants resident
at Tyn Court, just behind the square. In 1650 the
Czech sculptor Jiri Bendl erected the column of
the Immaculate Virgin (visible on the right), one of
the first Baroque monuments in Prague: four angels
fighting against the devil were portrayed around
the plinth, while the column was surmounted by
a statue of the Virgin Mary. The monument was
taken down on 3 November 1918, a few days after
the founding of Czechoslovakia; since 1990 an
organization has been working to restore it.

Marienbad, the Colonnade

Marienbad, a small town in Bohemia tucked into
a wooded valley, is sheltered by the hills and
forests of Slavkov. The site was occupied in the
fifteenth century by the monks of Teplá, who
first discovered a spring with curative properties.
Marienbad – Márianské Lazné in Czech – obtained
the official status of spa town only at the beginning
of the nineteenth century, thanks to the combined
efforts of Abbot Reitenberger and a doctor, Josef
Jan Nehr; and the first springs – the Krizovy
Pramen (the Kreuzbrunnen or Cross Spring),
the Marien Spring (once called the Salzbrunnen,
then the Marienquelle, from which the town
derives its name) and the Ambrozuv Pramen (the
Ambrosiusbrunnen or Ambrose's Spring) – were
opened to spa visitors in 1807 (Goethe visited in

1820). The Marien Spring possesses a gracious neo-
Baroque colonnade, built in 1889 by the Viennese
architects Hans Miksch and Julian Niedzielski.

Marienbad, Ambrose's Spring

'The autumn begins, and the trees turn yellow, red and brown; the little spa town, in its pretty valley, seems to be surrounded by fire. Beneath the arcades, women come and go and lean over the springs. These are women who are unable to have children and in these thermal springs they hope to find fertility' (Milan Kundera, *The Farewell Waltz*). In three lines, everything about Marienbad has been said: the place's beauty, the non-stop movement through the colonnades, and the hope for a cure. It is Czech writers (Kundera, and before him Kafka) or German writers (Goethe and Thomas Mann) who have best conveyed the ambiguous atmosphere of the spa towns, where illness is concealed behind a veil of society life. Ambrose's Spring, which is exceptionally rich in iron, was visited from the earliest days by those suffering from anaemia or, more often, tuberculosis – a common and often fatal affliction in the nineteenth century, which was to bring down Kafka, a Marienbad regular.

Hungary

Budapest, Clotilde Palace

Celt, Romanian, Magyar, German, Turkish, Austrian – all have
made Budapest the most exotic and perhaps the most oriental
city in Central Europe. 'The city of baths', 'Pearl of the Danube':
water has played an important role in the history of this great
metropolis, whose cosmopolitan atmosphere is freely expressed.
There are in Budapest as many Turkish baths as there are
Western-style thermal baths, and as many churches as there are
mosques and synagogues. After the union of Buda and Pest in
1872, under the Austro-Hungarian empire, the well-to-do middle
classes of Pest adapted themselves to the Austrian way of life, and
the city developed rapidly. Between 1872 and 1900 the station,
the university, the Parliament and the Opera all sprang up; and
the first underground train was built in 1896 (before the Paris
Métro) in time for celebrations to mark the millennium since
the arrival of the Magyars in Hungary. Wide avenues, squares
and Art Nouveau palaces were constructed. At the centre of this
image, extending beyond Szabadsjato Street, is the Elisabeth
Bridge: constructed between 1897 and 1903, it owes its name
to the Empress of Austria.

Bosnia

Village festival in Bosnia

In a big meadow, in a clearing at the edge of the forest, Bosnian villagers gather for a kermesse. This festival, which seems to have pagan origins, takes places every year on the third Sunday in October. Its name has been traced back to the Middle Ages, when Catholic priests turned general festivities into a celebration to mark the anniversary of a church's foundation. The kermesse is celebrated under different names in Bavaria, Saxony, Thuringia, Switzerland and Austria: the German word used here – Kirchweih – reminds us that Bosnia-Herzegovina had been under Austrian administration since 1878. These villagers from the 1890s, shown here in their Sunday best, are waiting for their fellows to return from the forest where they have gone to uproot the 'Kirchweih tree', which is to be replanted in a big hole dug for the occasion. The tree, which often measures some 30 metres (100 feet) in height, used to be pulled by a horse, or hauled by the young people themselves, up to the trench. If it withered, this would be taken as a very bad sign.

Sarajevo, the Turkish district

On a fault line between Rome and Byzantium, between East and the West, Bosnia has often experienced conflict through the centuries. The various Christian sects of Orthodoxy, Catholicism and Bogomilism (a heretical religion derived from the Gnostics) came into contact with Islam, which had been introduced by the Turks in the fifteenth century. The Ottoman empire, which controlled the country for three hundred years, left a deep mark on Bosnia. It is claimed that religious conversions to Islam were made easier by the fact that Bogomilism was a more 'permeable' faith than the others. It is also said that many Bosnians chose to convert in order to keep their privileges and property. The Turkish district of Sarajevo was effectively under Austro-Hungarian administration at the time this photograph was taken, but Bosnians of Slavic origin were no happier under the supervision of the Austrians than they had been under the Ottomans. Rising nationalism eventually led to a young Bosnian Serb assassinating Archduke Franz Ferdinand in Sarajevo, an event that triggered the First World War.

Sarajevo, the market district

A 1950s travel guide says the following about Sarajevo: 'It is the Orient, and it is Austria. The Orient can be seen in its minarets, its little winding streets that climb the wooded slopes; Austria in its straight roads and its fortresses that dominate the city.' But Sarajevo was founded by the Turks, and was the Ottoman empire's second city, called 'the flower among cities'. In the midst of this all-Oriental scene, dominated by the minaret of a mosque, with veiled women and turbaned men coming and going, the West remains a discreet presence, hinted at by the Neoclassical façade of the building visible on the left.

Young woman from Sarajevo

This young girl – photographed in a studio in front of a painted background, embellished for better effect with a sheep on a bed of straw – is very probably Muslim. Her wide, puffed-out Oriental-style trousers suggest this, and the red silk with which they are made indicates that they are for a festival. The cotton blouse with wide sleeves is a typical article of clothing, worn by all Bosnian women, not just by Muslims; but this one is elaborated with embroidery and lace. The braided corselet used to be worn also by Catholics and Orthodox, but the absence of a smock gives a further indication that this woman is Muslim. The girl's leather sandals are traditional , typical of every province of the former Yugoslavia.

The mountains of Herzegovina

From Lika and western Bosnia, the massif of the Dinaric Alps stretches all the way to Montenegro. This mountainous region, the 'Himalayas of Herzegovina', is a land where springs and green valleys alternate with steep, plunging gorges, waterfalls and immense forests of pine and fir trees. The country people of Bosnia-Herzegovina lived for a long time from hunting and fishing, trading wood and cattle-breeding. But in the southern part of the country, closer to the Adriatic coast, the climate is milder, and the mountains are more maritime in character, with fig trees, orange trees, cypress and laurels much in evidence.

Montenegro

The arrival of the post in Cetinje

'Almighty God, you would think you were somewhere on the moon!' cried Pierre Loti, struck by the view from Mount Lovcen, the bare, arid peak that dominates Cetinje, capital of Montenegro – the country of the 'black mountain'. In the 1890s, at the time Loti was visiting, the interest of this photographer was captured by the arrival of the post. At the time Cetinje was no more than a large town, and although its prince, Nicholas I (made king in 1910), tried to live a life there worthy of his crown, the arrival of the post was still a big event. If the Adriatic coast was no more than 45 kilometres (28 miles) away, under Austrian rule and very popular with visitors, the excitement did not extend as far as Cetinje.

Romania

Bucharest, monument to Michael the Brave

The Romanians' distant ancestors – the Scythians and the Agathyrsi, who exploited the gold mines of Transylvania – came down from the Carpathian Mountains to establish themselves between the Black Sea and the Danube. After the Roman Conquest came a period of one hundred and fifty years of intense population growth. Invasions by Barbarians, Tartars, Finno-Hungarians and Mongols followed – ten dark centuries when cities were razed to the ground and traditions were snuffed out. There was then a slow Vlach renaissance until the fourteenth and fifteenth centuries, when Turks occupied the Romanian provinces of Wallachia, Moldavia and Transylvania. Finally, around 1599–1600, Michael the Brave, the son of a Vlach father and a Greek mother, reasserted the independence of his country and made Bucharest his capital. For this reason the Romanian independence movement, still fighting in the nineteenth century, raised a monument to their national hero. For, although Turkish rule had ended, the Romanians suffered repeated attacks from Russians and Austrians. In order to take shelter from the threat of the Russian empire, they finally made an alliance with the Emperor Franz Joseph.

The Kazan Gorge

This inhospitable river on which a steamboat is sailing by, dwarfed by the towering rocks, is the Danube – a world away from its broad and majestic appearance in Vienna or Budapest. 'Father Danube' is shown here at the Iron Gate, a succession of wild gorges that hinders its progress between the Romanian Carpathians and the Serbian Balkans. The Kazan Gorge, the narrowest and most dangerous of them all, represents the last obstacle before Orsova and the plains of Wallachia. The Roman Emperor Trajan gave up all attempts to navigate the narrow passage with his ships, and raised a bridge across the gorge to penetrate into Dacia. And in the nineteenth century several projects – Hungarian, Serbian and Romanian – were planned to make the pass navigable. Between 1890 and 1896 an attempt was made to drive a canal through, which necessitated blowing up the rocks of Prigada and cutting into the mountain for some 2 kilometres (1¼ miles). The Sip Channel was opened on 17 September 1896 by the Emperor Franz Joseph,

Prince Carol of Romania and King Alexander Obrenovich of Serbia. Despite the huge efforts involved, the Iron Gate remained difficult to navigate, since the currents there were so strong. As late as 1970 boats going up the Danube were still hauled by locomotive! This was the case until 1972, when the gigantic Iron Gate dam was built at Djerdap.

Sinaia, the Crown Prince's hideaway

This tree house belonged to the reigning prince of Romania, Charles of Hohenzollern, the future Carol I. This den at the end of the park at Peles Castle was the sovereign's secret refuge from the glitter, hustle and bustle of the castle. King Carol adored nature and chose to live far from the dusty streets of Bucharest in Sinaia, a small village set in the foothills of the Carpathian Mountains. There, from 1875 to 1883 and from 1893 to 1914, he had an extraordinary castle built, with a multitude of towers and belfries, whose eclectic interior decoration variously evoked the German Middle Ages, the Renaissance and the Moorish architecture of Spain. It included marble, gold, stucco, panelling, frescoes, Aubusson tapestries, an arms room and a Turkish smoking room. At Peles, Carol and his queen, Elisabeth, led a life that was far from conformist. The queen, who was a writer, a champion of women's rights, and an able amateur in the world of the arts, used a pen name – Carmen Sylva – and was fond of wearing traditional Romanian dress.

She played the piano and organized musical and literary evenings, at which the participants included Pierre Loti and Sarah Bernhardt, the composers Paderewski and George Enescu, the violinist Pablo Sarasate and the Romanian poet Vasile Alesandri.

Turkey

Constantinople, Eminönü Port and Yeni Camii Mosque

'This view is so strangely beautiful that you wonder if it is real. You would think that you were looking at one of those opera backdrops made to decorate some Oriental extravaganza, and, thanks to the painter's imagination and the glow of the footlights, it shines with the impossible gleam of apotheosis' (Théophile Gautier, 1853). A short walk from the bustle of the Spice Bazaar is the Yeni Camii, one of the most important mosques in Istanbul, built on the banks of the Golden Horn. Next to the jetty at Eminönü, where the water all but disappears beneath a flotilla of caïques, the mosque's massive and imposing outline dominates the crowd flowing across Galata Bridge at the centre of the city, used every day by thousands of citizens.

Constantinople, Turks smoking in front of a café

Ottoman poets would sing of the 'four cushions of pleasure': tobacco, coffee, opium and wine. In 1555 two Syrian merchants, Hakim and Shams, opened the first coffee house in Constantinople and made their fortune from this beverage called the 'milk of chess players and thinkers'. According to the poets, it should be 'as black as the devil, as hot as Hell, as pure as an angel, as sweet as love'. Ever since its introduction into Turkey by English traders, tobacco has been considered the natural accompaniment to coffee. Everyone would come to the café with his pouch of tobacco, or *tombeki*; the *chibouk* (a long-stemmed clay pipe) or the *narghile* (a water pipe with more than one stem) were provided. Coffee houses spread throughout Constantinople and became places for all manner of idle discussions. The traveller could hardly be mistaken in assuming that 'everywhere the Turk finds himself, he will make his kif, that is to say, he will have his chibouk in one hand and his cup of coffee in the other, and he will be lost in some absorbing daydream' (Maxime Du Camp, 1848).

Constantinople, a fountain on Scutari Street

A district on the Asiatic coast, downstream along the Bosphorus, the ancient site of Chrysopolis ('city of gold') was renamed Scutari in medieval times. It was once the place where caravans from Anatolia would stop on their way to Constantinople, and from which pilgrims would depart for Mecca. At the centre of the Hakimiyeti Milliye Square near the docks (also called the Port of Scutari), a charming marble fountain was built, decorated with arabesques and Turkish inscriptions. It is dominated by the imperial mosque, constructed in 1548 by Sinan – the court architect appointed by Suleiman the Magnificent – for the Princess Mihrimah Sultana, his daughter.

Constantinople, an entrance to Hagia Sophia (opposite)

Literally 'street of the cold spring', the Sogukçesme Sokagi climbs the first hill of Constantinople – which has seven hills – alongside the enclosure of Hagia Sophia (into which one might enter via the roofed entrance seen here). Tourist guidebooks would recommend a walk along this delightful side street, which is lined with traditional wooden Ottoman houses, each built in a similar style, with projecting bays.

Constantinople, street scene before a mosque

The larger Ottoman mosques were not just places of prayer. Likewise the imperial mosques, which were integrated into a complex, called a *külliye*, that comprised a number of buildings with well-defined functions: a Koranic school, a library and a popular dining hall intended for the poor. In this period the mosque reached beyond its religious purpose to occupy a social and intellectual dimension, attested by the number of faithful gathered around the walls of this prayer hall, absorbed in their reading or in animated discussions.

Spain

Seville, Andalusians on horseback

The clothes of this Andalusian horseman comprise a leather jacket, a velvet waistcoat, gaiters open at the calf, a flat-brimmed hat and a red silk waistband. He is pictured probably at Alcalá de los Panaderos, a small town where the running of the *novillos* (young bulls) took place and to which aficionados would come from Seville for the occasion, as Théophile Gautier described in his *Journey to Spain* (1846). From the shallow, sandy banks of the river Guadalquivir, the Giralda (Seville's cathedral tower) can be seen on the left of the picture, pointing upwards into a sky heavy with heat, 'its colours of amethyst and aventurine not seeming compatible with our sad northern climate. The statue of Faith glitters at the top of the tower like a golden bee at the tip of a huge blade of grass.'

San Sebastian, the beach

In 1843 Victor Hugo described San Sebastian as
a city of poets and smugglers, ruined by civil war,
where 'one is born Basque, speaks Basque, lives
Basque and dies Basque'. Women no longer wore
mantillas during the summer in the Belle Epoque –
they traded them for straw hats or parasols; and the
more robust among them would take advantage of
their cabins on wheels to change for sea bathing,
but only at high tide, since at low tide half of the bay
would be left dry.

Barcelona, restaurant at Tibidabo

'At the ticket office of the Catalonian Railways,
I bought a third-class ticket to Tibidabo station. . . .
Taking refuge in the darkness of the tunnels,
I rested my head against the window while the train
journeyed through the bowels of the city to the foot
of Mount Tibidabo. When I re-emerged into the
streets, it seemed as if I were discovering another
place. Dawn was breaking and a purple blade of
light cut through the clouds, spraying its hue over
the fronts of mansions and the stately homes that
bordered Avenida del Tibidabo.' This description
of the climb up towards Tibidabo is taken from *The
Shadow of the Wind* by Carlos Ruis Zafón, a writer
born in Barcelona in 1964. But the development of
the site and its amusement park goes back to the
very beginning of the twentieth century: a doctor
from Barcelona, Salvador Andreu, financed its
construction, and the park was served by a funicular
railway that opened in 1901, at about the time that
this picture was taken.

Madrid, the Royal Armoury

The collection of the Royal Armoury, begun by
Charles I of Spain (Charles V of the Holy Roman
Empire), was moved to the Palacio Real in the
second half of the sixteenth century by Philip II
when he decided to establish his capital in Madrid.
Théophile Gautier visited the Palacio Real in 1846,
and found that the armoury was rather disappointing,
since the suits of armour on show were rarely
complete and made up a rather mixed assortment.
He noticed, for example, that 'helmets of an earlier
and later period were placed with cuirasses of a
different style'. The carriage that was claimed to
be Joanna the Mad's, mother of Charles, seemed
somewhat too recent to be convincing. Gautier also
regretted that there were too few Moorish arms –
'two or three bucklers, some yatagans, that was all' –
but was curious to note 'the embroidered saddles,
studded with gold and silver and covered with small
steel plates like scales, of which there are many and
in strange shapes'.

A bullfight

The first horseman to present himself in the ring,
ready to fight bulls from horseback, was probably
the eleventh-century leader known as El Cid.
These fights took place on rare occasions, 'for royal
marriages, when a treaty was to be signed, or when
a chapel in a cathedral was to be inaugurated. . . .
The noblemen, dressed in bright silks, would enter
the lists on their war horses and would attack the
animal with their lances. . . . If the bull succeeded in
unsaddling them, they would draw their sword, and,
with the aid of their lackeys, they would kill them in
one way or another. . . . When the festival was more
popular, it was the masses who would come down
into the arena and who would attack the animal all
together, until the creature succumbed to dagger
blows.' This extract is from *Arènes Sanglantes*
('Bloody Arenas', 1908) by Vicente Blasco Ibañez.
Horses were disembowelled and bulls were stabbed
through the heart (as many as six in a day), in an
arena marked out by the red circle of the barrera,
amid the exasperated shouts of the crowd.

The Feria de Seville

Elegant horse-drawn carriages make their way to
the fair, the gentlemen elegantly dressed and the
ladies wearing Parisian fashion but mounted on
superb Andalusian horses: this is the festival to beat
all festivals, the Feria de Seville, taken in about 1900.
'Nothing is so exciting, so arresting to the eye, as
the Seville Fair', wrote Charles Duvillier, who made
a journey around Spain in 1862 with Gustav Doré.
'Here, a *gitano* opens the mouth of a horse he is
about to sell, or shows off the fine shape of a donkey
or a mule; further along, a *majo* spreads out his
cloak like a carpet in front of a *maja* who is coming
towards him mounted on an Andalusian horse,
wearing a *sombrero calañés* on her head; there is
an urchin smoking a cigarette, or a *gitana* telling
one's fortune; then cows, sheep, the gaudily painted
calesas carriages. Shops, with pointed roofs, made
of planks and canvas, are lined up in long rows
from one end of the field to the other and laid out
with the most diverse range of goods imaginable;
the botillerias, where one may buy liqueurs and
iced drinks, are very numerous.'

Seville Cathedral, the Puerta del Perdón

Seville Cathedral was formerly the Grand Mosque,
built in about the year 1000. The western entrance,
known as the Puerta del Perdón ('Door of
Forgiveness'), is clearly of Moorish origin, despite
being decorated with statues of saints. Behind, we
catch a glimpse of the Patio de los Naranjos ('Court
of the Orange Trees') – another legacy of the original
mosque, planted with numerous orange trees in
serried rows.

Seville, the Alcázar (overleaf)

This is a view of a set of doors leading to the Patio
de las Doncellas ('Court of the Maidens') in Seville's
Alcázar. A masterpiece of *mudejar* workmanship,
the doorway is framed by white marble columns
and decorated with arabesques, ceramic tiles and
spectacular plasterwork.

Granada, the Generalife

A quarter of an hour's walk from Granada, the Generalife was the summer residence of the caliphs of Granada and part of the Alhambra Palace complex. This terrace, with its arcades and arabesques gleaming with whitewash, possesses the charm of remote places that have gradually become forgotten. It displays a typically Moorish aesthetic, having neither ostentatious decoration nor superfluous ornamentation, but the real wonder of the Generalife was – and remains – the extraordinary beauty of its gardens and water features.

Granada, Gypsy caves

The Gypsy way of life was accepted in Moorish Spain, but underwent a brutal change at the time of Ferdinand II, the king of Aragon and then of Castille (1474–1516). In 1499 the first persecutions took place, as a result of the Gypsies' nomadic existence being declared against the law. The Gypsies, many of whom lived in Andalusia, abandoned their towns and took refuge in the hills and caves. The Gypsy district of Granada is on the Albaicín hillside, where families gathered together in cave dwellings dug from the chalky rock. Obliged to settle in one place, the Gypsies became blacksmiths, mule shearers and horse dealers, while the womenfolk would tell fortunes and sell castanets and jasmine in the doorways of the Alhambra.

Málaga, the fishermen's meal

White sand as fine as dust, a sky veiled with a haze of
heat, bare purple mountains and the Mediterranean
as still as a lake. On the beach at Málaga, a group of
fishermen finish eating their midday meal while
others take a siesta in the shade of a boat. Every
Spaniard knows these lines of verse, taken from
Night Song of the Andalusian Sailors by Federico
García Lorca:

'*¡Ay muchacha, muchacha / Cuánto barco en el
puerto de Málaga!*'
'Oh! My girl, my girl / How many boats there
are in the port of Malaga!'

Gibraltar, the Rock seen from the road to Spain

Here is the potholed road to Spain used by travellers who had landed by boat and passed the British health inspection. Gibraltar, a British colony, is principally a mighty rock opposite the coast of Africa, overwhelming the village itself with its vast bulk. The sole passage between the Atlantic and the Mediterranean, the straits are so narrow that, when the weather is clear, boat passengers can see Cape Spartel and the Bay of Tangier. Moorish, Castillian, Spanish, and then acquired for the British Crown in the Treaty of Utrecht in 1713, the territory of Gibraltar is an incredible melting pot, where today the population comprises British, Moroccans, Andalusians, Portuguese, Maltese, Italians and Indo-Pakistanis. Although the official language is English, the Gibraltarians express themselves in *llanito* – a variant of Andalusian dialect. A third linguistic group speaks Moroccan Arabic, and the Spanish-speaking group is only the fourth largest community in Gibraltar.

Portugal

Porto, Ribeira Quay

In this 1890 photochrome of Porto, all the activity is concentrated in the foreground. At the bottom of the grey granite stairs, the big square-sailed boats of the Douro River, the *rabelos*, crowd against the Ribeira quay, where the open-air market is taking place. This is where fish was mostly sold in those days – sardines and cod brought in by the boats. Since the eighteenth century the first calling of the *rabelos* was not fishing but the transport of barrels of port wine, harvested on wine-growing estates of the Douro Valley and aged in the store houses of Gaia, the hillside on the right of the picture. Stretching between Vila Nova de Gaia and Porto, the impressive Dom Luis Bridge replaced the old pontoon bridge that was endlessly threatened by the rising waters of the capricious Douro River. The city's second bridge after the iron viaduct of Maria Pia, built by Gustave Eiffel, the Dom Luis Bridge was begun in 1881 by one of his disciples, the Belgian engineer Théophile Seyrig. After it was opened in 1886 by King Dom Luis I, it became the city's emblem.

Lisbon, the Tower of Belém

The tower of São Vicente de Belém at the mouth of the Tagus River was built in about 1550–20 by the military architect Francisco da Arruda. King Manuel I wanted it to guard the entrance to the port of Lisbon, and it carried the name 'sentinel of the Ocean'. But the tidal wave that followed the disastrous earthquake of 1 November 1755 – which destroyed 85 per cent of Lisbon – brought with it the accumulation of sand that connected it to the land. Having been miraculously saved, the tower lost its strategic position in a single day, and hence the reason for its existence. Bombarded in 1831 by the French navy, it could not prevent Admiral Roussin's fleet from forcing its way through the narrows and entering the port of Lisbon. During the decades that followed and until the end of the colonial era, the Tower of Belém was used as a garrison and as the Customs building. This picture, taken in about 1900, shows a legionnaire, easily recognizable from his *kepi*, apparently on the lookout for arriving ships.

Lisbon, fishermen in the port

At the port in Lisbon, at the beginning of the twentieth century, the fish sellers of the old town are sitting on their baskets, waiting for the daily catch to arrive and for the frantic fish auction to begin. Among them are many *varinas* (sardine sellers) from Alfama, who would walk tirelessly up and down the paved side streets of this working-class district, carrying heavy baskets of fish on their heads. Grilled sardines, which one eats accompanied by plenty of white wine, have always been a typical Portuguese speciality.

Italy

Venice, full moon on the Grand Canal

'Today I would like to tell you a little about Venice: these views
will give you the best impression', wrote Richard Wagner to
his wife, Minna, in 1838. 'I have enclosed the principal views
in colour, although these are not of works of art, but in Venice
lively colours play such a part that one could not truly picture
the city for oneself at all with no more than some simple black
silhouettes.' Théophile Gautier seemed to be in agreement,
writing in 1850: 'How can I describe these pinks of the Doge's
Palace, which seem to be as alive as flesh, the snowy whites of
the statues, drawing their curves against the azure of Veronese
and Titian, the reds of the Campanile as it caresses the sun, the
flashes of distant gold, the thousand views of the sea.' Here is a
view of moonlight on the Grand Canal, captured in 1900; in its
subtle colours it would have been unimaginable fifty years earlier.

Lake Como, Varenna

'Too beautiful!' said Hermann Hesse, of Lake Como.
'However, this time once again, the complete
beauty strongly attracted me and bewitched me:
the rocky romanticism of the villages hanging on
the shore, the seriousness and the confidence of
the aristocratic villas, with garden, park and port . . .
all of that sleeping in a cold silence worthy of a
fairy tale.' On the coastal path leading to a villa in
Varenna, a peasant is carrying a heavy load of wood.
Tall cypresses shade the terraces that tumble down
to the calm, cold waters of the lake. Mark Twain
was also bewitched: 'here indeed does distance lend
enchantment to the view – for on this broad canvas,
sun and clouds and the richest of atmospheres have
blended a thousand tints together, and over its
surface the filmy lights and shadows drift, hour after
hour, and glorify it with a beauty that seems reflected
out of Heaven itself' (*The Innocents Abroad*, 1869).

Lake Maggiore, Isola Bella

A beautiful Neoclassical building, the Villa Torrione
has been owned since 1856 by the Doria Lamba
family. On the Isola Bella – which Alexandre Dumas
found 'the most curious' of the Borromean Islands –
the garden terraces overlook Lake Maggiore
majestically. 'Everything there is made to measure,
marble and bronze, in the Louis XIV taste', Dumas
went on. 'A real forest of magnificent trees, a forest
of poplars and pines, these giants murmuring softly
in the lightest breeze. . . . Each terrace is a flowerbed
embalmed with a different perfume, in the middle of
which the orange blossom always predominates, and
is populated with gods and goddesses. . . . A truly
royal villa, filled with coolness, greenery and water.'
Today part of the island is reserved for paying guests;
and in the gardens a cypress that was planted in 1830
continues to grow.

Lake Garda, *water carrier*

'At about midnight, my host accompanied me to
the boat . . . and I left the shore with a fair wind',
wrote Goethe. 'At sunset, when the mountain loses
its steep appearance, and when the countryside lowers
itself more gently towards the lake, one can see in
a row . . . Gargagno, Bogliacco, Cecina, Toscolano,
Maderno, Gardone, Salò. . . . There are no words to
describe the grace of this rich and populous country.'
Lake Garda, the largest and the furthest east of the
Italian lakes, is indeed famous for its extraordinary
sunsets; this example, in rich photochrome, evokes
the celebrated phenomenon.

Milan, *Corso Vittorio Emanuele II*

In Milan in 1867, Mark Twain compared the rhythm
of life he found there with that of American cities:
'We begin to comprehend what life is for. . . . We
walked up and down one of the most popular streets
for some time, enjoying other people's comfort and
wishing we could export some of it to our restless,
driving, vitality-consuming marts at home.' This
view of the Corso Vittorio Emanuele II in 1900
still seems to correspond with what Twain felt thirty
years earlier. The scene is a peaceful one: the street
is bathed in a light softened by the shade of tall
façades; the women passers-by are talking quietly
in the middle of the street; the shops are asleep
behind their awnings in the afternoon heat.
At the end of the curving line of coloured canvas
the Duomo appears, with a pale pink halo against
a cerulean blue.

Venice, Rio di San Trovaso

'Leaning back among soft, black cushions he swayed
gently in the wake of the other black-snouted bark,
to which the strength of his passion chained him. . . .
But his guide seemed to have long practice in
affairs like these; always, by dint of short cuts or deft
manoeuvres, he contrived to overtake the coveted
sight. The air was heavy and foul, the sun burnt
down through a slate-coloured haze. Water slapped
gurgling against wood and stone. The gondolier's
cry, half-warning, half-salute, was answered with
singular accord from far within the silence of the
labyrinth.' So wrote Thomas Mann, in *Death in Venice*
(1912). The district of San Trovaso was where gondola
workshops could be found (today only one is left): in
Thomas Mann's time – and that of this photochrome
– there were 10,000 gondolas operating in Venice,
compared with 350 today. The workshop pictured
here is just behind a church dedicated to Saints
Gervasio and Protasio, whose names in the Venetian
dialect are elided to 'San Trovaso'.

Venice, Canale San Cristoforo

Behind a Gothic palazzo edged with greenery – the
Palazzo Dario, which is said to be cursed – white
marble steps lead from the brick arch of a bridge
down to the green waters of a narrow canal.
Gathered at the bridge are group of well-dressed
children, a black gondolier and his languorous
passenger (a splash of colour against the shady
bank), and just above, in the centre of the picture,
a young man staring into the lens.

Trieste

In 1900 Trieste was Austrian, and it was to remain
so until the end of the First World War. 'This city that
speaks a Venetian dialect, and this countryside that
speaks a Slavic dialect, have been placed in the trust
of an irreproachable Austrian bureaucracy, but one
that speaks German. A world . . . composed mostly
of aristocrats with fair-haired little girls who are
surrounded by governesses, Bösendorfer pianos,
old Viennese porcelain, Biedermeier furniture. . . .'
These are the words of Roberto Bazlen, a writer born
in Trieste in 1902, in an essay that he devoted to the
city of his birth. An enormous port for trade and
passengers, a city of import–export firms, Trieste was
at that time one of the most prosperous and opulent
towns in the whole Austro-Hungarian empire.

Tyrol, the Vajolet Towers

These strange mineral formations, the 'towers'
of the Rosengarten Massif, are in the Dolomites
of the Southern Tyrol, near the village of Tiers not
far from Bolzano. The highest of them, the Delago
Tower (2,790 metres, or 9,150 feet), takes its name
from Hermann Delago, an Austrian who climbed
it in 1895. Near the end of his life King Albert I of
Belgium, a keen mountaineer, had a refuge built at
the bottom of the towers. The Rosengarten Massif
has been a particularly popular area for climbers
since the end of the nineteenth century. Legend
has it that Laurin, King of the Dwarves, here built
himself a castle surrounded by a rose garden, in
which he hid the gold, silver and crystal that his
people had extracted from the rock. King Laurin
was rich and powerful, but he lacked a wife. Not able
to put up with this situation any longer, he abducted
Simhilde, the daughter of the prince of Bolzano,
who was betrothed to the valiant knight Dietrich von
Bern. The story ends well, since Dietrich succeeded
in thwarting Laurin's magic powers, and he won
back his fair maid. It is said that the tower is lit up
by the colour red because of the roses that Laurin
dropped behind him as he fled.

Pisa, the Campanile

'Who will ever be able to explain the deep, sad charm of certain cities that are almost dead?' Guy de Maupassant asked himself when he discovered Pisa on his travels in 1889. It is true that at first sight this famous leaning tower, with its galleries of white marble piled high in the middle of the Campo Santo, does seem on the edge of abandon. Maupassant went on: 'When one arrives on the edge of this wild, deserted field, enclosed by old walls . . . one stands there dumb with surprise and stirred up with admiration. . . . Behind the cathedral, the Campanile, eternally leaning as though it were about to fall, ironically disturbs the sense of equilibrium that we naturally possess'. A woman visitor who climbed the Campanile in 1860 perfectly exclaimed on 'the dizziness that takes hold of you the further up you go, beneath those covered galleries', and how your eyes, 'dazzled by the intensity of the light on a summer's day, take in the immense horizon that spreads out all around'.

Florence, the Duomo seen from the Palazzo Vecchio

'Above the folly of politics, and out of range,' wrote Stefan Zweig in 1932, 'the eternal panorama, the white domes, the delicate line of the hills of Tuscany continue to shine, like the precious pictures that have lain for hundreds of years in their cool shelters, rich with colours, intense joy of the soul. . . .' Here we see the brown roofs of Florence and the famous cupola of the Duomo described so many times by travellers. Taken from the square tower of the Palazzo Vecchio, this view is less usual than the wider panoramas shot from the Boboli Gardens or San Miniato. This photochrome of the city's historic heart, enclosed by its amphitheatre of green hills, is a perfect expression of the colours of the Tuscan capital.

Italy 217

Rome, Piazza di Minerva and the Pantheon

Behind the Pantheon, the 'temple to all the gods',
is the Piazza di Minerva, where the coachmen have
parked their carriages around the obelisk, perhaps
waiting for the end of mass, or for tourists to exist
the church of Santa Maria sopra Minerva. This
church houses relics of Catherine of Siena and of
the painter Fra Angelico. The obelisk itself was
sculpted in the sixth century BC and is supported
on an elephant carved by Bernini. According to
historian and politician Edgar Quinet, writing in
1832, 'There are three Romes: that of Antiquity, that
of the Middle Ages, and that of the Renaissance.'
So it is that, in this small Roman square, an Egyptian
obelisk, an ancient Roman dome, a church from the
Middle Ages and a Renaissance sculpture exist side
by side.

Rome, Trajan's Column and Forum

'I have been running all day, on the eve of
the Festival of St Peter. I have already seen the
Colisseum, the Pantheon, Trajan's Column, Castel
Sant'Angelo, St Peter's; and I don't know what else.'
Chateaubriand's words express just how much
Rome, with all its immensity and architectural
riches, is an exhausting city, where one ends up
wanting nothing more than the peaceful sight of
nature. This photochrome shows Trajan's Forum
(AD 111–114), dominated by the column that was
dedicated to the emperor in 113 to commemorate
his victories over the Dacians; behind them rises
the imposing Baroque mass of SS Nome di Maria,
a church erected in the eighteenth century by
Antoine Derizet.

Naples, Via Casanova *(preceding pages)* and Santa Lucia *(opposite)*

It goes without saying that visiting Naples is nothing like visiting Rome or Florence. Naples gives herself to those who arrive with a lightness of spirit and a sense of adventure. 'What discoveries can be made here, what surprises there are to savour, even today, wandering in a haphazard way around the streets and alleys of Naples!' exclaimed Paul Morand on a visit here in 1938. 'Not one of us knew the district of Santa Lucia, where these tall, dirty houses, fluttering with washing, seemed to have risen out of the sea.' Taken in 1990, this view of houses with cracked façades and ageless pink plaster, high windows with green shutters and ironwork balconies – where an array of carpets, rags and green plants is hung out – evokes the working-class character of Santa Lucia. The city's vitality is plain to see in the improvised spaghetti-eating competition, which takes place in front of a charming open-air kitchen.

Palermo, Monte Pellegrino

Here, a district of Palermo sits beside a calm turquoise sea. Small boats bob on the surface of the water, and two people standing on the rocks look out over the bay. Behind the buildings rears the hunchbacked outline of Monte Pellegrino – according to Goethe 'the most beautiful promontory in the world', and much admired by many Romantic writers.

Croatia

The road from Ragusa to San Giacomo

Under a hot Mediterranean sun, a cart climbs the hill from
Ragusa to San Giacomo along a road lined with aloes. With
its limited shade this arid landscape is typical of the southern
point of the Dalmatian coast. The rocky headland visible in the
distance, extending out into the Adriatic, is Ragusa, the former
name for Dubrovnik. The old town of Ragusa is where Romans
and Slavs united against continual attacks by Turks, Greeks,
Venetians and various pirates. A seemingly impregnable fortress,
Ragusa in the fifteenth century was a republic governed by a
senate. Diplomats before all else, the inhabitants had obtained
from the Holy See, in exchange for their undying faith, an
exclusive right to trade with the 'infidels', thereby ensuring
control of the treasures of the East. At the height of its glory,
Ragusa was in competition with Venice: it was the second port
of the Adriatic and a prosperous trading city, and its fleet sailed
the seas as far as the New World under the flag of St Blaise, its
patron saint. At the end of the nineteenth century Austrian
Lloyd's steamers lay at anchor at Gravosa, its outer harbour.

Ragusa, the Fountain of Onofrio

'When one has studied the history of Ragusa, one cannot enter the city with anything but respect', wrote a French journalist in 1874. At the heart of the city is the Stradone (Italian for 'big street'), a long paved street lined with granite houses, overlooking passages and steep steps that follow the slope of the hillside. At its entrance stands a fountain inspired by the Ottomans, the great Fountain of Onofrio. With its sixteen sides, basins and impressive dome, it was built in about 1435–40 by the Neapolitan architect and water engineer Onofrio della Cava, to complement the new aqueduct bringing water to the city from the river Dubrovacka.

Pula, the Temple of Augustus

Coming down the coast of Istria from Trieste, Pula (ancient Pola) is the first large town that one encounters. Arriving there by sea, one sees nothing but the docks of the arsenal at first, but once the visitor reaches the port a number of splendid ancient buildings become visible. Pula was a Roman city of some importance, as is testified by beautiful ancient remains such as the amphitheatre and the Temple of Augustus. When the Austrians fortified the port of Pula in the nineteenth century, they apparently uncovered large basins in which the Romans once raised lampreys, who had a marked appetite for succulent flesh, which was said to improve their taste. The more salacious guidebooks used to claim that these strange creatures were thrown slaves or live prisoners to feed on . . .

Salona, the necropolis

The history of Salona (or Solin) is linked to
Diocletian, the son of an emancipated slave from
this Dalmatian city who became a legionnaire
and was proclaimed emperor in Rome in AD 284.
He retired in 305 to the area where he had been
born, and had a monumental palace built with
stones seized from the tombs of Egyptian pharaohs,
reigning over his countrymen as a tyrant and
persecuting Christians without mercy. By a sort
of irony, under the protection of Byzantium Solin
became a great centre of evangelization, and
Diocletian's palace was turned into a cathedral.
The Christian necropolis shown here, just at city
gates, contains some of the finest examples of
early Christian sarcophagi.

The Grotto of Lacroma (Lokrum)

A short boat ride away from Dubrovnik is the
little island of Lokrum, where it is said Richard
the Lionheart found refuge after he was shipwrecked
on his way back from the Crusades. In the nineteenth
century the Archduke Maximilian Ferdinand von
Habsburg, the island's owner, seduced by the beauty
of the site and its luxuriant vegetation, had a villa
built for himself surrounded by wonderful gardens
filled with eucalyptus, cactus and succulents.
History does not relate, however, whether the
archduke visited this cave, which is strongly
reminiscent of the Blue Grotto at Capri.

Greece

Athens, Temple of Athena Nike

While the architecture of the Parthenon signalled the primacy of Athens in the fifth century BC, the tiny Temple of Victory, better known as the Temple of Athena Nike, shows a certain evolution in taste. In place of the majesty of great Doric buildings, the elegance and more modest proportions of the Ionic order began to be preferred. One French archaeologist writing at the end of the nineteenth century desribed how 'One must admire the temples of the Acropolis, in the plain setting where they flourished, beneath the hot sun that has gilded their marbles. . . . The Temple of Victory . . . shines like a shrine, at the very end of the terrace and so close to the edge that one is afraid one might see it crumble into the precipice.' The temple is constructed on a steep bastion that overlooks the entrance to the Propylaea on the Acropolis hill. All its decoration has disappeared, and only the frieze remains, a rare depiction of a historic event: the Greek victory against the Persians at the Battle of Plataea in 479 BC.

Athens, Piraeus

'Today,' complained Gaston Deschamps in the opening pages of his book *La Grèce d'aujourd'hui* ('Greece Today', 1892), 'those who are afraid of seasickness must buy their ticket in Paris, at the Gare de Lyon, cross Italy at full steam, embark at Brindisi on a Lloyd steamer, land at Corfu, take themselves and their trunks on to a Greek steamer that makes them pay for the charming brevity of the crossing . . . stop at Corinth . . . travel along a corniche by railway . . . and disembark in a pell-mell of people embracing one another . . . on the platform of the station for the Peloponnese, an ugly building in a waste land.' Arriving at Piraeus, one the other hand, 'is more in keeping with ancient traditions and arouses all kinds of exquisite day dreams. One can well imagine, sitting on the rear deck of a steamer that snorts, smokes and beats heavily around like a monster without a hint of elegance, the triremes, illuminated and decorated with flowers, rocking to

the songs of the triumphant athletes. If one wishes to see Attica in all its beauty, and with the grace of its swift freshness, one must enter the port of Piraeus on a spring day, at the very moment when the precociously warm air of the month of March brightens the dry, sandy hillsides with an early and light glow of green.'

Athens, the Acropolis and the Temple of Olympian Zeus

Jean-Alexandre Buchon, a journalist, historian and author of *Recherches historiques sur la domination française en Grèce* ('Historical researches on French rule in Greece'), travelled through Greece observing the customs of the local people. In Athens, in February 1841, he attended a Lenten festival that was taking place around the columns of the Temple of Olympian Zeus. All Athenians came down into the valley overlooked by the temple to feast, dance and sing. On the way there, Buchon contemplated the unreal setting of these celebrations: 'The Temple of Jupiter [Zeus] presents itself in the foreground with its powerful columns; then, a little further away, in the middle distance, and as though to serve as a frame, the Acropolis rises up, topped by the Parthenon, which offers us its outline in all its elegance and grandeur: further off still, on the left, is the Hymettus mountain range. . . . There is a harmony and burst of colour here that could be captured only by the brush of Claude Lorrain.'

Meteora, St Stephen's Convent (overleaf)

In the fourteenth century the monastic communities of Mount Athos were threatened by repeated attacks from Turkish pirates. Three monks – Gregory, Moses and Athanasius – left their monastery in search of a safer haven. Their peregrination led them to Thessaly, east of the Pindus mountains, to the base of some giant sandstone formations that had been sculpted by the wind and rain. First a wooden hut was constructed at the top of these rocks, then a chapel, then a monastery. In the fifteenth century twenty-four monasteries made up this community called 'Meteora' ('hanging in the air'). There could be no better retreat for these men than this: the way to the top is near impossible, and in order to receive materials and provisions the hermits devised a system of nets, ladders and winches. Matters changed slightly in the 1920s, when steps were carved into the rock, reached by means of light bridges that spanned the yawning gaps.

Algeria

Algiers, Moorish woman on a terrace

Above the Bay of Algiers, over which the sun is soon to set, thousands of whitewashed terraces slowly fill with people. Women walk out in groups, talking together on the low walls, stretching out lazily, deep in private conversation. Here, their faces are unveiled. They wear silk tunics drawn in at the waist, and their transparent gauze sleeves reveal the shape of their arms. If one is to believe travellers' tales from the last decades of the nineteenth century, men were not admitted onto these terraces. The woman and the young man shown here must therefore have been posed by the photographer, a common practice at that time for this sort of souvenir photograph.

The port of Algiers

Every traveller used to say that when one arrived in
Algiers by steamer in the 1900s, the surrounding
silence, broken only by the sound of the prow carving
through the water, was suddenly interrupted by noise
from the town – a hum of activity getting louder as
the ship entered the port. This photochrome shows
a view taken from the Admiralty building. In the
centre, the northern jetty encloses the basin of the
port, defined in the background by the arcades of
the promenade.

Algiers, the arrival of a steamer

The passengers on this steamer are disembarking –
not directly into the port, but into Algiers harbour.
Perhaps the ship is making no more than a short
stop here, or it may be too great a vessel to put
alongside the quay (ports were not always equipped
to receive the new 'giants' that belonged to big
maritime companies). In 1900 Algeria was a
very popular tourist destination: the General
Transatlantic Company, for example, opened hotels
and organized tours that included accommodation
and transport by sea.

Algiers, Red Sea Street

Two women completely covered in white veils are hurrying through the streets of the Casbah district. These alleyways are sometimes so narrow that houses almost join at the top and the sky can scarcely be seen. Maupassant wrote: 'The sound of sweet and wild music occasionally escapes from these houses, from which one often can see women emerging, a little awkwardly, hesitantly, in twos . . . their legs hidden beneath simple trousers of toile or calico, which reach down to their ankles; and one tries to make out their faces behind the veil that clings a little to the outline of their cheekbones.'

Algiers, Place du Gouvernement

A few walkers are crossing the sunny expanse of the Place du Gouvernement; others have stopped for a moment in the shade of the statue of the Duc d'Orléans mounted on his horse. 'There is silence at midday in the Place du Gouvernement', wrote Albert Camus in 'L'Eté à Alger' ('Summer in Algiers', 1936). 'In the shade of the trees on one side, the Arabs are selling glasses of iced lemonade, perfumed with orange blossom water, for five centimes. They shout:

"Cold, cold!" and the word rings out across the empty square. After the noise of their cry subsides, silence falls again, as the sun beats down: in the drink-seller's jug, the ice is turning round and round, and I can hear the tiny sound it makes.' Emphasizing the impression of heat with its snowy whiteness, the Djemaa Djedid Mosque occupies one side of the square. On another side are arcades and awnings lowered over the front of a European café. This is summer in Algiers.

Algiers, Luce Ben Aben school of embroidery (overleaf)

Théophile Gautier, who visited Algiers in the 1860s, remarked on the skill of the city's young lacemakers and embroiderers. 'Between their fingers, threads of gold, silver and silk are interwoven without ever becoming tangled', he wrote. It was a skill that they learned very early on, like the little girls shown in this picture, taken at the Luce Ben Aben school.

Biskra, the market

In the heart of the Aurès region, the Biskra oasis is a frontier post and the gateway to the Sahara. Here, in Berber land, live the Shawia – they tend flocks and are descended from nomadic livestock farmers. At Biskra market, vegetables, aromatic herbs and fruits are for sale: figs, pomegranates, apricots and dates with amber-coloured flesh, which grow in abundance in the fields and orchards of the oasis, where the cool water favours cultivation.

Biskra, the old town

In the world of literature Biskra is linked to André Gide, who was fond of wandering in the old town, as was the hero of his short novel *L'Immoraliste* ('The Immoralist'). The work was written in 1902, making it exactly contemporary with this photochrome. Dressed in blue like men of the desert and driving his donkey in front of him, an inhabitant of Biskra is walking along the soft grey clay wall that follows the course of a stream, benefiting from the shade it offers. All the streets of the old town are squeezed between high walls with palm trees rising up from behind them; water flows through the middle, clear and blue.

Tunisia

View of Kairouan

In the middle of the desert, Kairouan, the holy city of the
Maghreb region, rises like a mirage. The first city in North Africa
to be built by the Islamic conquerors, Kairouan was one of the
biggest staging posts of the Muslim world. Caravans on their way
to the south of Tunisia would stop there, visiting the holy well en
route. This photochrome is a view from the minaret of the Sidi
Okba Mosque – one of the most venerated sanctuaries in Islam –
which rises above the flat roofs of the old capital. On the horizon,
the violet line of the Djebel Zaghouan mountain range divides
the earth from the sky.

Tunis, El Marr Street

The babouche souk, the fez souk, the perfumers'
souk, the copper souk, the cloth souk . . . the souks
of Tunis have been famous since the thirteenth
century. At the end of El Marr Street is the shady
entrance to one of these bazaars, full of evocative
smells and crowded with figures milling around.
El Marr Street continues on the left towards the
Casbah; the minaret and the dome of Sidi Mahrez
Mosque in Bab Souika Square are visible beyond.

Tunis, Sidi ben Ziab

Established as a small Berber town on a hillside
above Lake Bdira ('the little sea'), the rebel town of
Tunis was taken over by the Arab leader Hasan Ibn
Nooman in the seventh century. He built an arsenal
and a mosque: Jama Ez Zitouna, also called the
Mosque of the Olive. In the twelfth century Tunis,
capital of the Hafsid dynasty, became a flourishing
port and a cosmopolitan city, where sailors and
traders from Genoa, Venice, Spain and elsewhere
met to do business. This picture shows one of the
typical streets of the Medina of Tunis leading to the
Jama Ez Zitouna Mosque. The Zitouna is the seat of
the Muslim university and houses its library.

Tunis, Moorish café in Halfaouine

In the working-class district of Halfaouine, men use cafés as their traditional meeting places. They sit on mats or wooden benches, not necessarily eating or drinking, but smoking Arab pipes. In the evening during Ramadan, the cafés are swarming with people and are full of life. Acrobats with shaved heads, fire-eaters, dancers and musicians appear in the square until dawn prayers.

Arab dress in Tunis

Silk waistcoats made of brightly coloured material and edged with embroidery, and an assortment of turbans and embroidered belts. 'In this maze of narrow streets . . . this population moves around, seething and swarming, the most colourful, varied, draped, dressed-up, shimmering, silken and decorative crowd of the whole eastern shore. Where are we?' asked Maupassant.

Morocco

Tangier, two Arabs

In the photographic vocabulary of the twentieth century, the category of 'types' or 'studies' occupies a place all of its own. Filed under this classification are character portraits that used to be called 'exotic' – a euphemistic term for 'ethnic' – and various genre scenes. This picture might well fall under this category, since these two figures, dressed in their long *burnous* and mounted on their small Arab horses, are part of the collective imagination associated with the Maghreb. The sand, the sun on the horizon, the white foam on the sea, the solitude of these two men, their tall shadows falling on the sand: these elements bring to mind the legendary East and the dreams of desert adventurers.

Tangier, Cap Spartel

The first Moroccan town on the northern coast of
North Africa, Tangier has welcomed great numbers
of tourists every winter since the nineteenth century.
According to Pierre Loti, writing in 1889, so many
arrived in Tangier that 'the Sultan of Morocco has
decided more or less to give it up to visitors, to turn
his face away from it as though from an infidel city'.
On the dusty road leading to Cap Spartel, about
12 kilometres (8 miles) away from Tangier, a man is
resting under a tree, perhaps waiting for the heat to
abate so that he can continue on his journey.

Tangier, the Casbah and the Law Courts

The sense that we are looking at a deserted town
in this picture of the Casbah from about 1890 is
enhanced by the angle from which it was taken:
the eye is drawn to the emptiness of the foreground,
then funnelled towards the end of the street, where
a black doorway opens into shadow. The hurrying
people in the foreground seem unaware of the
camera's gaze. Only the beautiful ochre colour of
the building on the left lends the picture a little life.

Madeira

Funchal, woman in a hammock carried by porters

Off the coast of Morocco, in the Atlantic Sea just north of the Canaries, lies the archipelago of Madeira, and on the biggest island – Madeira Island – is Funchal, its capital. Much of the island is wonderfully verdant, rich with subtropical vegetation and terraces that slope down to the sea. In Funchal, formerly a British territory that was one of the country's favourite winter holiday destinations in the nineteenth century, Empress Elisabeth of Austria owned a villa; it was from Funchal that she embarked for her new palace in Corfu, the Achilleion. Apart from wicker-seated toboggans that pulled brave tourists to the promenade at Monte, on the hillside above Funchal, there was another charming mode of transport on the island: a hammock carried by porters. Dressed in white and wearing boater hats, the Funchal porters would carry upper-class tourists in them, mainly women. Made from strong canvas, the hammock was hung from a long pole carried on the shoulders of two men.

Canary Islands

Tenerife, the Bon Repos Hotel, Güímar

Continuing down the Atlantic coast of Africa, not far from the
south-western shores of Morocco, are the Canary Islands, seven
islands that the ancient Greeks called 'the Fortunate Isles'.
This name may be a little optimistic, since the climate and the
vegetation are practically the same as those of Africa, notably the
western Sahara. This photochrome may contain a backdrop of
green mountains, but if you look a little closer you can see that
they are fairly lightly covered, and the black soil of the terraces
in front of the hotel is clearly volcanic. Not a drop of rain was
recorded between 1871 and 1879, nor between 1958 and 1961,
when much livestock had to be evacuated to Africa. This hotel in
Güímar, on the island of Tenerife, had a particular reputation for
excellent French cuisine.

Egypt

Cairo, the Pyramids

From his post at the port in old Cairo, the French writer Edouard Schuré compared the three pyramids of Giza to three tents, 'unchanging in their triangular form, sentinels of stone showing the way to Upper Egypt'. He was not, of course, alone in praising these incredible golden structures and the vast tableau in which they feature – the incandescent sky, the palm trees reaching into the air, the fertile river and wide, majestic banks, and the arid desert that stretches out on all sides.

Port Said, the Arab district

Port Said was founded in 1859 by the Suez
Canal Company to house the workers who were
digging the canal, which opened ten years later.
This feat of engineering was a colossal enterprise,
requiring abundant manpower from all over the
Mediterranean, recalling the methods that the
Pharaohs employed when building the Pyramids.
At the end of the nineteenth century Port Said,
the vestibule of the Far East, had become a
cosmopolitan port where all the maritime powers
had their consulates. By virtue of its origins, the
city has kept some of its appealingly ephemeral,
transitory architecture – particularly in the Arab
district, which resembles a forgotten stage set,
with its houses and apartments cluttering the
urban fabric in completely random fashion.

Suez Canal, a ship and a dredger

The Suez Canal is hemmed in by very high sand
embankments, where no vegetation can survive
the salty environment. Big ships pass through it
every day (about fifteen a day in the 1920s), led by
dredgers that would laboriously clear sand from the
bottom. For its creator, Ferdinand de Lesseps, who
had obtained the trust of the Said Pasha, this 160-
kilometre (100-mile) canal – dug through complete
desert and linking the Mediterranean with the Red
Sea – was intended to halve the journey to India. But
the enterprise also depended on a gamble, which
eventually paid off: the rise of steamships from the
1870 onwards. Great Britain, whose reputation as a
sea power was second to none, became the principal
shareholder of the Suez Company at around the
same time.

Cairo, Mameluk tombs (overleaf)

In the course of a morning excursion to the
Mameluk tombs, Louise Colet, a French journalist
working in Egypt, was struck by the grandeur
and desolation of Cairo's Mameluk necropolis:
'The minarets and the domes gilded by the sun
are outlined in all their various forms. The finest
details of the sculptures are scoured by the light
and stand out clearly. The big edifices, in the solitude
of the desert, completely take hold of one's soul.
It is as beautiful and desolate as the Forum at
Rome, but vaster still, more imposing, more deeply
melancholic by being isolated from all contact with
the city, by the complete absence of all human noise,
and also by the forgottenness and nothingness that
have submerged the memories of these factious
sultans whose names no longer find so much as an
echo in their magnificent necropolises.'

Cairo, Kasr-el-Nil Bridge

In the nineteenth century the inhabitants of Cairo would make small trips to the enchanting island of Zamalek in the middle of the Nile, which was reachable only by boat. At the end of the 1860s Ismail Pasha commissioned the island's development, shoring up the embankments to protect against flooding and constructing a quay to facilitate access. At the centre of the island he built a palace surrounded by a botanical and zoological garden, with numerous pavilions and fountains. This palace soon became Ismail Pasha's favourite retreat, and the island very fashionable. Nonetheless, it could be reached relatively easily thanks to the revolving bridge of Kasr-el-Nil, built in 1872. Sometimes the bridge would open (as here) to allow several feluccas to pass through – those emblems of the Nile that have sailed up and down the river since time immemorial, transporting fishermen, travellers or goods.

Cairo, the mausoleums of Salar and Sanjar al-Jawli

Located in the district surrounding the very ancient Mosque of Ibn Tulun, the funerary complex of the Mameluks Salar and Sanjar al-Jawli, built in 1304, includes two identical mausoleums, under whose domes the two men are buried. In Egypt, Islamic monumental funerary architecture takes the form of independent mausoleums on square ground plans, covered with a dome and erected within the fortified walls of the town. It was Mameluk architects who first constructed domes in ribbed, sculpted stone with ribs, as here, and who devised three-stage minarets (a cylinder on top of an octagon on top of a cube). At the beginning of the twentieth century, the scholar Hermann Thiersch claimed that this design was a conscious recall of the lighthouse of Alexandria – a theory that has been strongly contested.

Cairo, a Bedouin and his wife coming back from market

The description of ethnic stereotypes had been a recurring theme in travel literature since the eighteenth century. At the heart of the Egyptian populace was the Arab labourer, or *fellah*, as distinct from the Arab of the desert, or *Bedouin*. A nomadic people from the centre of Arabia, the Bedouin have spread in successive waves across the Middle East, North Africa and Egypt. They subsist by raising and selling livestock, and participating actively in the local economy. Their clothing most often consists of a shirt drawn in at the waist by a large leather belt, over which they throw a coat of brown and white striped wool. Sandals and a turban are also usually worn.

Cairo, a fountain in the Arab district

Mameluk in origin, the *sabil* is a public fountain – here in the form of a kiosk – designed to offer drinking water freely to passers-by. In Arabic, *sabil* means 'the alms given to the man that passes', and according to Islamic custom to have a fountain built is an act of philanthropy. The cistern is filled with water from the Nile, and behind the screens a man would hand out copper cups of water.

Cairo, small trades in the backstreets (preceding pages)

Two charming glimpses of Cairo street life at the turn of the twentieth century: on the left, women sell cane sugar, whose juice is thirst-quenching; and on the right, two water-sellers do their rounds of the dusty alleyways, leaning forward to pour water out of the urns they carry on their backs.

Philae, the Temple of Isis from the south-west

At Aswan, gateway to the Nubian desert, the sacred
Nile abandoned its peaceful course: its riverbed with
hazardous stones and reefs made the water choppy
and navigation difficult. And, for the Belle Epoque
traveller who wished to visit the sacred island of
Philae, the Nile crossing turned into a sporting
descent of the rapids. Nevertheless, the English
novelist Amelia Edwards, who visited in 1873–74,
described how 'The approach by water is quite
the most beautiful. Seen from the level of a small
boat, the island, with its palms, its colonnades, its
pylons, seems to rise out of the river like a mirage.'
The Temple of Isis dates from the time of the
Ptolemaic Dynasty and the Roman emperors. Here,
in a view from the south-west, the columns of the
eastern portico lead to the entrance pylon, whose
monumental doorway can be seen on the left. Behind
this colonnade is the Kiosk of Trajan, which was
used to store the boat sacred to Isis when it returned
from visits to neighbouring sanctuaries. In the late
1970s the whole temple complex was relocated to
avoid flooding caused by the Aswan Dam.

Karnak, the Great Hypostyle Hall of the Temple of Amun (opposite)

Alongside the Great Sphinx and the Pyramids at
Giza, Karnak remains the most visited Egyptian
site. The colossal proportions of the Hypostyle
Hall and its columns with their papyriform capitals
never fail to astonish visitors. This view shows the
hall still buried under feet of rubble. The English
photographer Francis Frith emphasized the difficulty
of taking an image of this structure on account of the
narrow arrangement of the pillars: 'The impression
that the builders have wished to obtain, it seems,
by this remarkable assembly of enormous columns,
is the combined effect of immensity and power –
almost of terror – which penetrates the spirit when
you stand in the middle of them.'

Israel and Palestine

View of Lydda

This view through the twisted branches of an olive tree shows the
town of Lydda (present-day Lod). A former Greek colony, Lydda
(whose name appears in the Bible) became an intellectual rallying
point for Jews after the destruction of the Temple of Jerusalem in
AD 70. In the Middle Ages, the town was affected by the Crusades,
captured in turn by Saladin and then by the Crusaders. Richard
the Lionheart held the place in particular reverence: some
legends have it that St George, patron saint of England and slayer
of the dragon, was born here. A city with a strong Palestinian
Arab majority, Lydda went through a dramatic period at the time
of the creation of the state of Israel, in 1948. It was attacked by
Israeli forces during the Arab–Israeli War: many civilians were
killed and tens of thousands were forced to leave their homes.

Jerusalem, the Bazaar

'Oh! Jerusalem, holy for the Christians, holy for the Muslims, holy for the Jews, from which there rises the endless sound of lamentations or prayers . . .' These few spontaneous words by Pierre Loti speak of the eternal paradox of this legendary city and of the land that has never found peace. At the heart of the bazaar in Jerusalem, the late nineteenth-century traveller found himself transported to the medieval East. Nothing has changed in this picturesque crowd who invaded the market place every day: Bedouin proudly carrying amphoras or baskets of fruit on their heads, or driving placid camels laden with produce dug up from neighbouring mountains.

Jerusalem, the Antonia Tower

The Antonia Tower belonged to the fortress of the same name in which rebel Jews barricaded themselves in AD 70 during the Sack of Jerusalem and the destruction of the Temple. It dominates the Via Dolorosa, whose path, it is argued, follows the Way of the Cross taken by Christ to Golgotha. 'We were standing in a narrow street, by the Tower of Antonio. "On these stones that are crumbling away," the guide said, "the Saviour sat and rested before taking up the cross. This is the beginning of the Sorrowful Way, or the Way of Grief." The party took note of the sacred spot, and moved on' (Mark Twain, *The Innocents Abroad*, 1869). To judge from the entrance to this dark and unwelcoming little street, the reader will understand Mark Twain's disenchanted tone of voice as his guide marched him round all the holy places of Jerusalem, combining a high moral tone with tales of superstition and legend.

Jerusalem, three elderly Jews

This triple portrait is perhaps not very flattering, but it is representative of the times, when the Dreyfus Affair divided France and anti-Semitism in Europe was much in evidence. There are many elements here – such as the men's rigid postures and miserable clothing – that would have corroborated the prejudiced accounts of travellers who made their 'pilgrimage' to Jerusalem.

Jerusalem, the Wailing Wall

The only surviving remnant of the Temple of Jerusalem destroyed in AD 70, the Western Wall – also called the Wailing Wall – fulfils the role of an outdoor synagogue. Since the Ottoman era this has been the holiest site in Judaism, where groups meet here to pray or to celebrate religious festivals. The faithful write their prayers on pieces of paper and insert them in cracks in the wall.

Jerusalem, the Dome of the Rock (overleaf)

Built on the ruins of the Temple, Haram al-Sharif is the third-holiest place in Islam. Intended to proclaim symbolically the superiority of Islam in the Holy City, the Dome of the Rock, built in 688–91, is situated in the middle of a vast rectangular esplanade reached by eight staircases, each punctuated by an arcade. Left of the Dome of the Rock is the little Dome of the Chain, whose faience decoration surpasses its neighbour's in beauty. The sacred Rock beneath the Dome's gilded copper roof is said to be where God ordered Abraham to sacrifice his son Isaac, the point from which Mohammed left the earth for his nocturnal journey, and to have formed the foundation of the Holy of Holies of Solomon's Temple. Mark Twain, not much impressed with all these references, exclaimed: 'In the place on it where Mahomet stood, he left his foot-prints in the solid stone. I should judge that he wore about eighteens.'

Jerusalem, stone-cutters

In their timeless way, these stone-cutters are the
descendants of those who took part in building the
Temple in the time of Solomon: 'And King Solomon
raised a levy out of all Israel; and the levy was thirty
thousand men. . . . And Solomon had threescore
and ten thousand that bare burdens, and fourscore
thousand hewers in the mountains; besides the chief
of Solomon's officers which were over the work,
three thousand and three hundred, which ruled over
the people that wrought in the work. And the king
commanded, and they brought great stones, costly
stones, and hewed stones, to lay the foundation of
the house. And Solomon's builders . . . did hew them,
and the stone squarers: so they prepared timber and
stones to build the house' (Kings 1: 13–18).

Jerusalem, the Church of the Holy Sepulchre

The double doorway that serves as the entrance of
the Church of the Holy Sepulchre – the supposed site
of the Crucifixion, the burial and the Resurrection
of Christ – has been blocked up on one side since
Saladin took Jerusalem in 1187. So complex is the
agreement by which the different Christian
denominations administer the church that changes
to its fabric can be made only with great difficulty.
The ladder that sits under the right-hand window
in this photochrome was placed there sometime
in the first half of the nineteenth century; but since
the doors and window ledges are designated as
'common ground', no one has dared move it, and
it can be seen in the same position to this day.

Bedouin women

These young Bedouin carrying their children appear to have stepped right out of the orchards of Nablus, but the composition was more likely shot in a studio. The photograph has a somewhat ethnographic feel to it, and these two women are clearly being presented as 'exotic'. The face of the woman on the right bears the marks of a traditional Bedouin tattoo.

Jaffa boatmen

Until relatively recently, travelling via Jaffa (modern Haifa) was the usual way for Western pilgrims to approach Jerusalem. The dock at Jaffa was the worst on the coast, since in bad weather boats could not get close: 'The boat dropped anchor in front of a line of reefs. It is right that the Holy Land should be difficult to reach, and that, since the Middle Ages, going to Jaffa should be synonymous with running a risk. When modern industry has succeeded in changing these reefs into a straightforward port, when one may moor at Jaffa just as one would at Le Havre or New York, that will be the end of the austere beauty of Palestine', declared the French writer Edouard Schuré in 1898.

Lebanon

The Anti-Lebanon Mountains

From east to west, the terrain that lies between Lebanon's Mediterranean coast and the mountains on the Syrian border is very diverse, ranging through coastal plains, hospitable valleys, and lofty peaks. The Anti-Lebanon Mountains form a natural border with neighbouring Syria; running for approximately 150 kilometres (93 miles), the range reaches its southernmost point at Mount Hermon, which rises to 2,814 metres (9,232 feet). Crossing the region left a great impression on Mark Twain: 'We have [walked] across chalky hills barer and gorges drier than Syria herself could offer', he wrote. 'Everywhere the air trembled in the heat. In the gorges the burning atmosphere almost suffocated us.'

Panorama of Beirut

After the undulating, suffocating mountains of Anti-Lebanon, Beirut, like Damascus no more than twenty-five kilometres (15 miles) away, offers visitors a cooler prospect. The city stands on a hill sloping gently down towards the sea; the flat roofs of some houses are used as terraces where inhabitants may find fresh air coming off the sea when the burning desert winds are blowing. In the distance the harbour can be seen, sheltered by a spit of land that protects it from rough winds. The whole city is richly planted with trees – mulberry, fig, carob, plane, orange and pomegranate – which provide this scene with a vibrant green backdrop.

Syrian Muslim women in Beirut

'In the East, richness and beauty seek the shade; nowhere does one find the grand display of our luxurious exterior: the houses, like the women, are veiled. The women walk in the street with their face covered by a thick muslin veil, their shape obscured by the fullness of their dress. Their feet are wrapped in formless little boots; beneath this envelope, the most ugly resembles the most beautiful. But if one lifts the veil and tears away the dress, what wonderful *houris* emerge from this shapeless chrysalis!' (Charles Reynaud, 1846). Such sentiments were a commonplace facet of Orientalist writing in the mid-nineteenth century, though thankfully little expressed now.

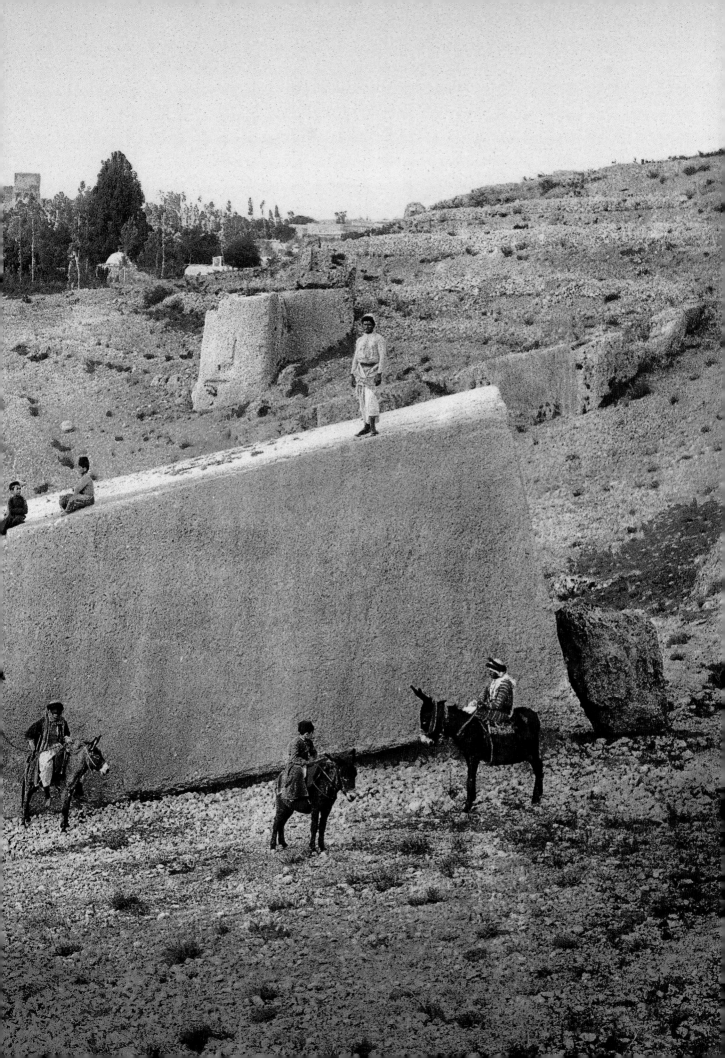

Baalbek, the Stone of the South
(preceding pages)

A Phoenician city dedicated to the sun god Baal, Baalbek became known as Heliopolis ('City of the Sun') under its Ptolemaic rulers. It became a Roman colony in 15 BC, soon after which several major temples – to Jupiter, Venus and Mercury – were planned and constructed. Over the following centuries the city was enriched by successive rulers, but eventually fell into disrepair, repeatedly damaged by wars and earthquakes. It was the publication of Robert Wood's *Ruins of Balbec* two years before the great earthquake of 1759 that truly popularized these colossal ruins for intrepid European travellers. The enormous block shown in this image, thought to be the largest hewn stone in the world, sits where it was cut almost two thousands years ago.

Baalbek, the Temple of Jupiter

On 8 June 1867 Mark Twain set sail for Europe and the Near East. His programme was to report back on the first organized tourist trip from America for the readers of *The Alta Californian* newspaper. Having crossed the Lebanese plains, Twain's caravan reached the ruins at Baalbek. The author was immediately struck by the vastness of these blocks of stone – 'as large as an omnibus' – which lay tumbled around the ancient site in a picturesque scene of decay and abandonment. 'What a wonder of architectural beauty and grandeur this edifice must have been when it was new! And what a noble picture it and its statelier companion, with the chaos of mighty fragments scattered about them, yet makes in the moonlight!'

Baalbek, a leaning column at the Temple of Jupiter

The French poet Alphonse de Lamartine expressed a similar admiration to Mark Twain when he visited Baalbek in 1832: he found 'something that no pen, no brush could describe. . . . Some of these desert monuments appeared intact, and seemed just to have emerged from the hands of the workman; of others only the remains were still standing, some isolated columns, some leaning wall sections and some dismantled pediments: the eye roamed freely among the sparkling colonnades of these varied temples, and the height of the horizon prevented us from seeing where this stone population ended.'

Syria

Damascus, Bab al-Saghir cemetery at Midan

In Muslim towns, the term *midan* refers to a large open space
where horsemen could train. South of the ramparts of Damascus
is a district known as Midan, where every year there is a pilgrims'
procession. A short walk from here is the Bab al-Saghir cemetery,
the biggest in Damascus, recognizable by its little green domes.
It has been used by Muslims since the seventh century and
houses the tombs of many caliphs and savants. Tradition has it
that many companions and descendants of the Prophet are also
buried here. Shi'ite tombs can be recognized by their flat upper
surface, while Sunni tombs are rounded like camel humps.

Damascus, Straight Street

The streets of Damascus for the most part follow ancient Roman roads, which explains their straightness. The most famous of these, Straight Street, which is also Damascus's principal street, crosses the city from west to east for more than a kilometre (½ mile), linking Bab al-Jabiya and Baba Sharqi. The buildings with colonnades that line the street at the beginning soon give way to businesses, shops and houses. Surveying the city in 1867, Mark Twain followed the length of Straight Street and commented ironically on its name: 'The street called Straight is straighter than a corkscrew, but not as straight as a rainbow.' The Ottoman governor Midhat Pasha used the least expeditious methods for renovating the street at the end of the nineteenth century, setting fire to the district's narrow streets so that he could redevelop the area as he chose.

Damascus, a palace courtyard

Enclosed by high windowless walls, typical Damascene houses include a central courtyard around which all the rooms are arranged, as in ancient Roman villas. The Azem Palace, constructed in 1750 for an Ottoman governor of the city, follows this traditional groundplan but is constructed in a much more opulent fashion, with its alternating bands of black basalt, white limestone and pink sandstone. In the eighteenth century Damascus had over one hundred and fifty palaces.

View of Damascus

Generations of writers have praised this city, which stretches along the cool waters of the river Barada like an oasis in the desert. The English traveller Alexander William Kinglake visited Damascus in 1834, describing it as 'a city of hidden palaces, of copses and gardens, and fountains and bubbling streams. The juice of her life is the gushing and ice-cold torrent that tumbles from the snowy sides of Anti-Lebanon. Close along on the river's edge, through seven sweet miles of rustling boughs and deepest shade, the city spreads out her whole length. As a man falls flat, face forward on the brook, that he may drink and drink again, so Damascus, thirsting for ever, lies down with her lips to the stream and clings to its rushing waters.'

Syrian Bedouin herdsmen

'I come through the long suburb of Meidan beneath a sky of immortal youthfulness, passing long lines of camels and Bedouin, armed with lances or rifles, amid this smell that is very particular to towns of the East, a little sickening and filled with appealing images – here, images with animal strength, ephemeral beauty, proud and dirty barbarism. The Arabs of the desert have been coming to Meidan since the beginning of time to buy and to sell. Many of them appear for two or three brief visits in their whole lives, without knowing what era we are living in, or what the world consists of. In the middle of this seething crowd, there they are, on their own, sitting on a low platform, a faraway fatalistic look in their eyes, or perhaps in a circle of ten or twenty of them, taciturn and noble' (Maurice Barrès, 1923).

Sri Lanka

Colombo

This scene probably shows the heart of the old centre of
Colombo, the Pettah. This district, which in former times
is where Dutch citizens lived, is a collection of shops and low-
built houses, and lively streets crowded with traditional carts
covered with coconut mats and drawn by little *zebu* cattle.
The Tamils of Ceylon (present-day Sri Lanka, off the south-east
coast of India) were recognizable by their rudimentary clothes,
bare chests and turban-like headgear. They were often unskilled
labourers, referred to as 'coolies', who carried out all kinds
of manual work on the roads and in the plantations, bringing
in the harvest or transporting goods.

Galle, Temple of the Buddha (overleaf)

The gleaming white dome of the Temple of the Buddha shines
amid the exuberant vegetation of Ceylon. This *dagoba*, known
elsewhere as a stupa, is a Buddhist commemorative monument
that often houses a relic. Its dome, the *anda* ('egg'), which once
sparkled with gold and precious stones, is set on a terrace and
surrounded by a colonnade with several entrances. At the top
of the dome, set on a quadrangular elevation, is the *khota*: a little
cone that is sometimes gilded. The last vestige of the Portuguese
colony at Galle – the bell tower of a Catholic church – is integrated
in the Buddhist temple enclosure.

India

Southern India, temple dancers

Among the eight classical styles of Indian dance, the *Bharatanatyam* is the most perfect. It originates in the south of India, and its name comes from *Bharat*, the Indian word for the country itself, and *natyam*, which means 'dance' in Tamil. It was once practised exclusively in temples by *devadasis*: these were dancers who had a hereditary attachment to the temple, having been dedicated to the god in childhood. The dance offering, an act of devotion, was codified in the *Natya Shastra* (a treatise on the dramatic art of dance) in the first century BC; and its aesthetic and choreography inspired many sculptures on the walls of temples. At the beginning of the twentieth century the *Bharatanatyam* was saved from oblivion and adapted for the theatre.

Madurai, gopura

'In Madurai, a city that was once the capital of
a wealthy king, there is a temple dedicated to Shiva
and Parvati, his consort, the fish-eyed goddess;
the temple is bigger than our Louvre, infinitely more
finely carved, more sculpted and perhaps more filled
with wonders. . . . Half-naked men come and go, their
hair ruffled from washing, their eyes both dreaming
and at prayer. The sacred elephants, the sacred cows
that live in the dark naves, the birds in the sky that
tuck themselves away in the towers, at different
levels of the red pyramids, all of this quivers and
moves about in the morning brightness'. Contrary
to Pierre Loti's enthusiastic report, the enclosure
of the extraordinary double temple of Meenakshi-
Sundareswarar in fact covers an area only half as big
as the Louvre. The sanctuary is, however, famous for
its eleven *gopuras* (gateways), all abundantly covered
in sculptures of gods and characters from Hindu
mythology.

Bombay, the University

'Here there are corners of London, corners of
Benares, corners of Shanghai. . . . I can see antique
carts pulled patiently by slow oxen in the midst
of tramways, victories, palanquins, porters' chairs . . .'
– so wrote a visitor to Bombay in 1891. At the end
of the nineteenth century Bombay was undergoing
great economic expansion and becoming more
involved in international trade, owing to the export
of cotton from Gujarat. The presence of the British
was visible everywhere: in the names of streets, the
design of gardens, and particularly in the Victorian
public buildings, such as the Gothic-style University
(seen here in about 1900). Bombay has now become
Mumbai, after the name of the Hindu goddess who
protects the city, and the streets and squares have
traded their colonial names for names in Marathi.

Agra, the Red Fort

Shah Jahan (1592–1666) was responsible not only for the Taj Mahal at Agra. It is to him that we owe most of the monuments constructed within the Red Fort, the fortress that his grandfather, Akbar, had erected between 1565 and 1574 as a symbol of Mughal greatness. Behind the walls 'the colour of blood oranges', one can get 'a glimpse as if of Alhambras through white lace, like palaces in a dream. . . . It was there that the Great Mughals lived with their sultanas . . . inaccessible and hidden in the middle of the whiteness and transparency of pure marble' (Pierre Loti, 1903). The esplanade of the Hall of Public Audience (Diwan-i-Am) – visible on the right – could be reached via an elephant ramp. Here imperial durbars took place, which brought together great dignitaries from around the kingdom.

Lonavala, Karla Caves

The prayer-hall of this sanctuary, carved out of a hillside by Buddhist monks in the first century before the birth of Christ, and whose bare style evokes the sobriety of a Cistercian monastery, is one of the most remarkable specimens of religious rock architecture. Pierre Loti wrote: 'Some men long ago, who had a dream that was as terrible as it was colossal, worked unrelentingly over many centuries to carve [the caves] into the granite mountains. . . . In around the year 1000 of our era . . . they were already at the height of their glory, and from every corner of India a constant stream of countless pilgrims came to visit.'

Delhi, Qutb Minar

In 1900 Qutb Minar was the tallest minaret in the world, standing at 72.5 metres (238 feet) high. According to a contemporary guidebook, 'only the Eiffel Tower can give an idea of the impression one gets standing at the bottom of the red sandstone monument'. It was erected in 1192 by Qutb ud-din Aibak to mark the victory of this Muslim sovereign over northern India. The illusion of height is exaggerated by the way in which the cylindrical shape tapers towards the top. Its ornamentation is also striking: the décor of fluting and arabesques becomes more developed as it climbs the tower, and each stage is overhung by a massive balcony in sculpted relief. The summit, which is reached by an internal spiral staircase of three hundred and ninety-nine steps, offers an unimpeded view over the whole plain and the city of Delhi.

Delhi, Chandni Chowk district

Chandni Chowk is the commercial district of Old Delhi. It was a long, narrow, lively street lined with many shops. From saris to kitchen utensils, via a whole range of spices, ivory and perfumes, almost everything was for sale and ready to be haggled over. Pedestrians, cyclists, horse-drawn carriages and, today, motor cars and trucks fill the streets where ox-drawn carts used to have right of way.

Jaipur, the Maharaja's Palace

The capital of Rajasthan, the 'country of kings',
Jaipur is the work of Jai Singh II, the astronomer
prince, who in 1727 entrusted his plans for a new
city to a Bengali priest initiated into the secrets of
sacred architecture. It was not until the Prince of
Wales's visit to India in 1876 that the city was clothed
in its incomparable pink colour. In our own time
the writer Paul Mann has described the Maharaja's
Palace as 'a majestic ensemble of towers, turrets
and crenellations that commanded the pass three
kilometres away, as theatrical, as improbable as a
children's picture book. . . . When the car stopped,
a little sentry door opened, and from it emerged a
servant dressed in a tunic and turban. . . . The three
visitors went through the door in single file. They
found themselves in a dark, vaulted tunnel lined
with the empty stalls of what had once been the
palace bazaar. It was here that long ago the
maharaja's wives and concubines – of whom he had
almost two hundred – would have come to buy their
jewels, perfumes and silks. This gallery smelled of
ancient and abandoned places.'

Gwalior, Teli ka Mandir

Legend has it that the town of Gwalior was founded
in the eighth century in homage to the hermit
Gwalipa, who cured the rajah of leprosy. Perched on
a sandstone cliff looking down on the town from a
height of 100 metres (330 feet) is the famous fortress
of Gwalior, reached by two ramps carved out of the
rock. The fortified plateau is covered with palaces
and temples built by the former kings of Gwalior,
among which stands Teli-ka-Mandir, the 'temple
of the oil merchants': a massive construction with
unusual barrel vaulting that is believed to have been
dedicated to a cult of the Mother goddess.

Benares, the ghats (overleaf)

Those who bring their life's journey to a close at
Benares (modern Varanasi), the holy city of Shiva,
are most fortunate: their soul will depart directly to
paradise. The ghats – the steps that line the banks
of the Ganges where cremations and ritual ablutions
of the faithful take place – number sixty-four in total,
the number of completeness. Having paid their fee
to the Brahmins, who crouch beneath vast parasols
and give them certificates of purification, beads,
amulets and other indulgences, pilgrims bathe in
the sacred water, preferably when the sun sends its
first rays over the horizon.

Calcutta, on the Hooghly River

'At last we arrive at the mouth of the Hooghly, and its waters are filled with the earth brought by the Ganges and the Brahmaputra from the plains of Hindustan, from the slopes of the Himalayas. . . . On the river, large boats pass slowly, powerful steamers whose port of origin is in England, America, Australia': so wrote a French traveller in 1891. It is on the banks of the Hooghly, one of the tributaries of the Ganges that empties into the Bay of Bengal, that the city of Calcutta was born. Originally there were three villages – Kalikata, Sutanuti and Govindapur – on the shore of the river. On 24 August 1690, Job Charnock, a functionary of the British East India Company, received permission to build a factory at Sutanuti, and in 1698 the Company obtained the right to collect land taxes from the towns. From this came the idea to merge the three towns into one,

which was named Calcutta (or Kolkata). The city's subsequent commercial success was largely thanks to its port on by the Ganges delta, which guaranteed a safe mooring for ships. Calcutta was the political capital of the British Raj until 1911.

Calcutta, the ghats

As at Benares, several quaysides in Calcutta have
been turned into ghats, some of which (the 'burning
ghats') are devoted to cremation. Others, such as
the one in this picture, are reserved for bathing.
Hindus traditionally come every morning in order
to cleanse their body ritually in the sacred Ganges.
Here, the men have finished their ablutions and
are resting under a beautiful cast-iron colonnade.
They are being groomed by barbers and are giving
one another massages. When the sun was too high,
big canvas shades were drawn down in front of
the arcades.

Singapore

Kampong Bahru, near Singapore

In 1826 the towns of Singapore, Malacca and Penang were joined together under the administration of the British East India Company and were thereafter known as the 'Straits Settlements'. In 1867 they became colonies of the British crown. An exceptional conjunction of events – the opening of the Suez Canal in 1869 and the development of steam navigation – established Singapore as a successful port. Here is a remarkable image of two worlds coexisting: opposite the harbour of the port of Singapore, full of steamships from all over the world, are the timeless *kelong* (fishing platforms) and *kampong* (villages) of fishermen's huts on stilts.

Singapore, the Cavenagh Bridge

The only suspension bridge in Singapore, which links the north bank of the Singapore River with the commercial district on the south bank, this is also the oldest bridge in Singapore conserved in its original form. Before it was built, one would have had to make a detour via Elgin Bridge or pay one duit to cross the river by boat. Designed by the colonial Public Works Department, the Cavenagh Bridge was constructed in Glasgow – where it was tested to support a load of four times its own weight – and transported in pieces by boat, to be reassembled on arrival in Singapore. Named in honour of William Orfeur Cavenagh, the last governor of the Straits Settlements, Cavenagh Bridge was opened to traffic in 1870. Rickshaws and ox carts became more and more numerous, and soon the bridge was barely able to cope with the traffic. In 1910 the government decided to build the larger Anderson Bridge, converting the Cavenagh Bridge for pedestrian use.

Singapore, Tanglin Road

A ubiquitous symbol of the Far East from Pondicherry to Singapore, the *jin-riki-sha*, or rickshaw, is a handcart that comprises a chair on two wheels, protected by a hood and manoeuvred by one or sometimes two people. A light and swift means of transport, it is ideal for negotiating crowded streets – or for losing oneself in an immense forest of bamboos. These are the botanic gardens in Singapore, whose luxuriant vegetation grows far above the Tanglin Road.

China

Peking, the Summer Palace seen from the east

Under the Qing dynasty, the imperial gardens experienced a new golden age, in particular during the reign of Qianlong (1736–99), sometimes called the 'gardener emperor', whose passion for the art of gardens became a way of life. Around Kunming Lake, which takes up two thirds of the area of the Summer Palace, Qianlong further developed the 'Gardens of Perfect Brightness', which had been planted in the reign of Kangxi (1662–1722) and which would be partly destroyed during the sacking of the Summer Palace in 1860. In this picture, the two principal components of the Chinese garden – hills and water – can be seen: the lake with its sinuous contours and the rocks worn into strange shapes. These are also the components of landscape painting, and are believed to encourage meditation.

Peking, the Summer Palace and the Jade Belt Bridge

Lining the western shore of Kunming Lake are six bridges, of which the most beautiful, curved like a ribbon, is the Jade Belt Bridge (Yu Dai Qiao). Made from white marble and granite, it allowed the imperial family's boat to pass beneath it, since they used this route to cross Kunming Lake on the way to the Jade Fountain. It is accessible only on foot, and the acute angle of its arch means that one has to ascend a flight of stone steps to cross.

Peking, the Summer Palace and the Marble Boat

Emperor Qianlong ordered the construction of the Marble Boat in 1755 to signify that the Qing dynasty was as solid as marble and could not be overturned. After its destruction in 1860 by occupying Anglo-French troops, the Dowager Empress Cixi, appropriating money collected to renovate the Chinese navy, had the boat rebuilt out of marble in a Western style. Measuring 36 metres (120 feet) long, its upper part resembles a projecting pergola, while the lower part – decorated with painted bricks, multicoloured glass and mosaics – recalls the paddle steamers of the Mississippi. Cixi used to take tea on this 'Boat of Purity and Ease' eternally moored to the west bank of Kunming Lake.

New Zealand

West Coast, Kotau Point

With its 700 islands and 15,000 kilometres (9,500 miles) of coastline, wherever you find yourself in New Zealand you are never far from the sea or the mountains – the reason why this country's geography is so spectacular. The West Coast of South Island, which today constitutes the Westland National Park, is the wildest. Described by Captain Cook as an 'inhospitable coast', it remained uninhabited for a long time, until the Greenstone Creek delivered its first flakes of gold in 1864. This 'desert with a threatening sky and an impenetrable forest' was very quickly invaded by prospectors, who made the region more welcoming. The coast of Westland near Knights Point is very impressive: seen from the air, the coastal plain of the Haast River, one of the most beautiful areas of the country, looks like a maze of wooded dunes and scattered lakes.

Auckland, view from St Matthew's Tower

The city of Auckland is built on an isthmus so
regularly penetrated by estuaries and creeks that
it is almost an island. At its narrowest point it is
1.3 kilometres (0.8 mile) wide, and a good walker
can apparently cross the city in twenty minutes.
It was William Hobson, New Zealand's first
governor, who founded the new British colony of
Auckland in 1840, naming it after George Eden, the
1st Earl of Auckland. At the time, land transactions
were made in an atmosphere of great confusion and
misunderstanding: the colonists believed that they
could profit by offering the Maoris several Western
comforts (blankets, trousers, rifles), while the
Maoris, ignorant of the notion of individual property
ownership, believed they were letting their land for
rent. A number of land transfers were thus the
subject of conflict between Pakeha (Europeans) and
Maori, some of which are still being contested today.

Westland, Mahinapua Creek

A tropical atmosphere pervades this forest of
kahikateas (white pines) and rimus (red pines)
stretching to the south of Westland. Mahinapua
Creek, a real floating forest, is the perfect spot
for fishing or for a leisurely boat ride. One could
also travel down the river by steamboat as far as
Mahinapua Lake, following in the tracks of the gold
prospectors of Hokitika, the city whose 'streets are
paved with gold'.

Milford Sound, Mitre Peak and Sinbad Gully

On the West Coast of the South Island are some of the most sublime landscapes one could ever wish to see. The region of Milford Sound was for Rudyard Kipling 'the eighth wonder of the world'. The panorama speaks for itself: a deep fjord at the foot of a steep rocky pyramid, the Mitre Peak – so called because it resembles a bishop's mitre – which reaches a height of 1,692 metres (5,551 feet). The valley of Sinbad Gully is the last refuge of the very rare owl parrot, or *kakapo*, the only flightless parrot in the world. In 1860 explorers of the West Coast complained that they could not sleep because of the booming nocturnal mating call of the male bird. Twenty years later the space was threatened by an invasion of ships' rats, which originally arrived with Cook's ships. Today Sinbad Gully is closed to visitors in order to protect its threatened fauna.

Whakarewarewa, Wairoa Geyser

For pioneers newly come ashore onto North Island,
the Rotorua region must have resembled hell:
'Walking across this land that is mined with fire, one
is constantly haunted by the fear of dying a lobster's
death. . . . Holding onto a Maori's arm, you squint
into the gulf gaping at your feet ready to swallow
you up' (Baron de Hübner, 1886). During a visit to
one geyser in 1934, the infernal atmosphere made
George Bernard Shaw remark: 'Hell's Gate, I think,
is the most damnable I have ever visited, and I'd
willingly have paid ten pounds not to have seen it.'
These volcanic phenomena – which are responsible
for giving North Island its nickname, the 'Smoking
Island' – have attracted curious tourists and spa
visitors since Victorian times. A few kilometres
from Rotorua, the thermal zone of Whakarewarewa
has the most impressive geysers: some eruptions
climb to a height of 60 metres (200 feet) and last
for several seconds. The unbeaten record is for an
eruption that occurred on 8 January 1903 that lasted
for more than two hours.

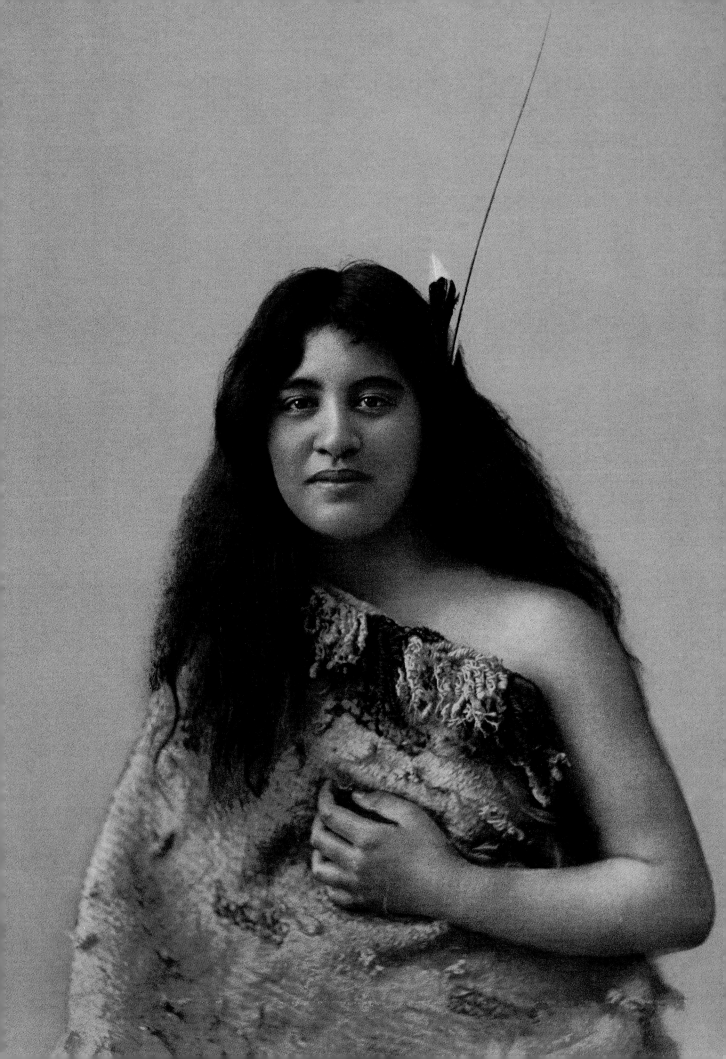

A Maori girl

The *moko*, or face tattoo, has a special meaning
for the Maori. A mark of elevated social status for
a man, it is allowed only for women who are 'under
a husband's authority', who can then choose to
emphasize their lips with the colour blue or to tattoo
their chins. It is forbidden to young girls, whose
unstained lips allude to their virginity. Respectful of
tradition, this young girl wears female ceremonial
dress: a wrap of *harakeke* (*phormium tenax*, or New
Zealand flax) with a decorative fringe (*taniko*), and
a bird feather (*huia*) in her hair. In Maori society it
is the women who work with supple materials: they
weave flax leaves into wraps and baskets, or, once
they have softened them in thermal springs, make
fabric for ceremonial garments. Soaked, kneaded
and bleached, the flax leaves produce a dense fibre
that can be used for ropes and in the construction
of houses and canoes.

Lake Te Anau, southern fjord

Lake Te Anau stretches for 120 kilometres (75 miles)
from Milford Sound on the south west of the South
Island, and after Lake Taupo is the biggest lake in
New Zealand (it covers 344 square kilometres, or
133 square miles). Three majestic fjords carve into
its banks, which shelter numerous endangered
bird species. New Zealand is a country of grand
panoramas, and this sunset over Lake Te Anau
confirms this reputation. 'The lake is vermilion,
lightly silvered matt gold. At the end of the land,
towards the north-west and making a frame for this
shining sheet of water, crenellated mountains, of
a transparent black, stand out against the sky that
is orange at the bottom and then pink, then higher
up pale blue. The nuances inbetween are beyond
description' (Baron de Hübner, 1886).

Canada

Quebec, Dufferin Terrace and Château Frontenac

Arriving from the United States by train – and in the early 1900s there was scarcely any other practical means of transport – one had to cross the St Lawrence River at Lévis to reach the city of Quebec. This view, showing the Dufferin Terrace and Château Frontenac, is almost what Stefan Zweig would have seen when he visited in March 1911 – except that Quebec was then under a layer of snow. 'And how wonderful to see this immense river frozen into a giant block of ice from one bank to the other!' Zweig exclaimed. 'Large steamers are imprisoned in a green blanket, and smaller sailing boats are covered in a layer of ice right to the very tops of their masts, as if enveloped in a sheet of glass ... I know of nothing more moving in our vision of today's world than these remote linguistic islands that have remained faithful for hundreds of years, and that are now quietly crumbling away'. Zweig's sensitivity was admirable, but his pessimism was misplaced: Montreal, capital of the province of Quebec, is today the second most important Francophone city in the world.

Quebec, Rue Sous-le-Cap

In the Lower Town, running along the Old Port
district, the Rue Sous-le-Cap is the narrowest street
in the city of Quebec. Since the waters of the
St Lawrence River used to flood it regularly, the
street was paved with wood, which was more
resistant than stone. A network of little footbridges
(an example can be seen in the picture) criss-
crossing from one house to another allowed
people to keep their feet dry in times of flooding.

Montreal, Place Jacques-Cartier

The Place Jacques-Cartier is still the liveliest area
in Old Montreal today. At the turn of the twentieth
century a big market used to be held here, to which
country people came in from neighbouring villages
to sell their grain, honey, beer and farm products.
The Place Jacques-Cartier still occupies a special
position in the historic heart of today's 'shopping
capital': in the summer, musicians and magicians
perform on the terraces in front of the restaurants
where snails are served (in the French tradition).
The white marble column that can be seen in the
background is thoroughly English, however: it
was erected in 1809 to commemorate Nelson's
victory over Napoleon at the Battle of Trafalgar
four years earlier.

Montreal, Château Ramezay

This unpretentious building is Château Ramezay, the residence that Governor Claude de Ramezay had built for himself in 1705. It then belonged to the East India Company, became military quarters and law courts, and then returned to its role as the Governor's residence once again. The château was put up for sale by the government in 1893, and narrowly escaped the demolition men's pickaxes thanks to the powerful Montreal Society of Archaeology and Numismatics, which acquired it from the City on the promise that they would turn it into a museum, a portrait gallery and a library. So it was that the museum – now the oldest in Quebec – was born. Château Ramezay houses a collection of 30,000 objects – manuscripts, printed matter, medals, works of art, stamps and furniture.

Niagara Falls in winter, Canadian side

For an average European of the end of the nineteenth century – or indeed an American citizen of Miami or Dallas – to receive a photochrome such as this from a travelling friend must have made quite some impression, evoking all the drama of the 'sublime' scenery of North America. Apart from the majestic spectacle of the frozen waterfalls – which in itself is breathtaking – the photochrome technique has captured the winter sun lighting up the upper cataract with its reddish glow, illuminating the virgin snow and the curtains of falling ice.

United States

Colorado, Devil's Gate Bridge on the Georgetown Loop Railway

'I like America, I like its imposing nature, its powerful mountains, its majestic rivers, its thundering waterfalls, its vast lakes, its endless prairies, its forests decked in eternal green. . . . I follow the progress of tireless explorers with admiration, who, in the ice of the North Pole, in the burning plains, in the snowy mountain ranges . . . cross over the frontiers of the new world in every sense. . . . Finally, with lively interest I see these passionate fighting people . . . who make one wonder what sort of role this magnificent country will play one day, in the forces of the globe'. This touching homage was made by a nineteenth-century French geographer, just one of many Europeans attracted to this vast new world. Georgetown in Colorado was a boom-and-bust town that had first come into being with discovery of gold in 1859. The development of the railroads in the 1870s and 1880s also established the town on the tourist agenda for those who sought the rugged romance of the Rocky Mountains. Railroad excursions took in the scenic Georgetown Loop, which guidebooks and postcard views helped to popularize.

Arizona, Thanksgiving dances at Old Oraibi

Old Oraibi, founded in about 1150–60, is the oldest village in the United States. Until 1907 it was a centre for the Hopi people, a peaceful and sedentary community of pueblo Native Americans who were always in dispute with the Navajo, a nomadic warrior tribe that came down from Canada and that today constitutes the most important Native American community. The celebration of Thanksgiving was not a traditional Hopi custom, but presumably encouraged by Christian missionaries. Such outside cultural influences eventually led to religious discord, and those more open to the new ways founded a breakaway settlement, New Oraibi, in 1890. Now based in a reservation within Navajo Country, south-west of the Grand Canyon, the Hopi people continue to practise their ritual ceremonies,

fire dances, eagle dances and snake dances, and try to maintain a distance from visitors. The plate from which this photochrome was taken dates from 1874, and is attributed to William Henry Jackson, one of the pioneers of American photography. By 1877 Jackson had amassed over one thousand negatives, a selection of which he published in his *Descriptive Catalogue of Photographs of North American Indians*. He left his entire collection of negatives to the Detroit Photographic Company, distributor of photochrome pictures in the United States.

Arizona, Grand Canyon
(above and overleaf)

By the end of the nineteenth century the Grand Canyon in Arizona was already a tourist attraction; in 1892 the first hotel was opened there, and in 1901 the Grand Canyon Railway was completed. It was probably in about 1883 that William Henry Jackson photographed the tourists shown in this picture, coming down the zigzag trail from Bright Angel Canyon guided by a cowboy. Bright Angel Canyon leads to O'Neill's Point – one of the best observation points of the Canyon. Of the incredible view available from this lookout point (overleaf), an American author, John McCutcheon, wrote that he 'stopped open-mouthed with amazement to see this frightening immensity and the peaks of these

gigantic mountains painted in all the colours of the rainbow'. Some visitors have suffered from vertigo and have fallen to their knees, while others have burst into tears. It is said that an engineer who came along as a tourist one day, astonished to see a cavity 21 kilometres (13 miles) in circumference by 1.6 kilometres (1 mile) deep, offered to fill it for a dollar per cubic yard. The Grand Canyon of Arizona became a National Park in 1919 and can claim to be one of the wonders of the natural world.

Ojibwa Indian, called 'Arrowmaker'

'The Americans do not know what to make of this
truly wild race that has remained so inscrutable after
two centuries of efforts and evangelization', noted
the writer Jules Huret on his return from America in
1908. 'They do no more than push them back more
every year towards the desert west . . . they give them
land that is worse and worse; [the Native Americans]
are obedient but complain bitterly.' The Ojibwa lived
on the border with Canada, by St Mary's River in
Michigan, on the western shore of Lake Superior.
They fished and traded in furs, coming and going
across the rapids in their canoes.

Yellowstone Park, Sapphire Hot Springs

Yellowstone is the oldest National Park in the United
States, created in 1872, more than forty years before
the Grand Canyon was granted the same status.
The region had in fact been explored since 1806,
the year of the Lewis and Clark expedition, and then
in 1807 by John Colter. But no one believed Colter
when he described the geysers and the sulphurous
springs whose fumes rose from several basins.
Sceptics ironically dubbed Yellowstone 'Colter's
Hell', so improbable did this tale seem to them.
It was the photographs of the Mammoth Hot
Springs by William Henry Jackson – commissioned
by the US Geological Survey, a section of the
Department of the Interior in Washington, D.C.,
in 1870–71 – that provided proof of the existence of
these exceptional natural phenomena and made
Congress designate Yellowstone a preserved site.

Cowboys and gold prospectors of Colorado

Here is a sequence devoted to the principal
characters of the historic West: the cowboys and the
gold and silver prospectors. For those who wanted
to head for the West, driving cattle was a good way
of earning money while they travelled to their
destination. Once they had arrived, many cowboys
'changed hats' and bought a gold-prospector's kit –
which they could resell in case of necessity. One
traveller made a note of a message he discovered
stuck to a wall by an unlucky worker near Ouray in
Colorado: 'I've got no more work, I have to leave,
I want to sell: 1 bed with iron springs, 1 desk with
secret drawer that makes a good strong box, 1 anvil,
1 vice, 1 bucket, 1 hammer for breaking rocks,
3 prospector's picks, 1 set of hair-clippers.'

Cowboys and gold prospectors of Colorado (continued)

On this double page are scenes from the lives of various Colorado adventurers, from the lassoing cowboy top left to the men who are loading silver ingots in the bottom right-hand picture. The original plates from which these photochromes were made were taken by William Henry Jackson in 1866 and 1867 when he was himself a cowboy, leading herds of cows and horses from Wyoming to Colorado to earn enough money to open a photographic studio in Omaha, Nebraska.

Colorado, the Midland Railway in snow

The conquest of the wide open spaces of America
inevitably followed the advance of the railroad: once
the pioneers had opened the way, businessmen
invested in railroad companies and the engineers
did the rest. The case of the Colorado Midland
Railroad (later Railway) was no exception. The
line was constructed between 1883 and 1893 by
the engineer John J. Hagerman. Forcing a way
across the Rockies, it linked Colorado Springs with
Leadville – a silver-mining town – crossing passes
at altitudes of more than 3,000 metres (9,850 feet).
In the winter such journeys could be particularly
dangerous, and wooden shelters like the one visible
here were built as protection from avalanches.
Locomotives were fitted with turbines that performed
the duty of snow ploughs. The Colorado Midland
Railway changed ownership several times until its
final bankruptcy in 1917.

Oregon, the Cascade Rapids

The Columbia River, the fourth-largest river in North America by volume after the Mississippi, the St Lawrence and the Mackenzie, flows out into the Pacific Ocean in the north of Oregon, where it defines the border with Washington State. A short distance before the mouth of the river, at a place called River Gorge, these rapids (known as the Cascade Rapids or Casade Falls) constituted a significant hazard to navigation. In his account of the first expedition on the Columbia River in 1806, the explorer Meriwether Lewis wrote that the team had to take their canoes to the rapids, unload them and carry their trunks for more than 2 kilometres (1¼ miles) in torrential rain, on a rough, slippery road that ran alongside the river. It was also necessary to watch the camp very attentively, since 'many of the natives crowded about the bank of the river where the men were engaged in taking up canoes; one of them had the insolence to cast stones down the bank at two of the men'. Numerous conflicts blew up between the Native Americans of the Cascades and the fur-traders who came down from Fort Vancouver (in the neighbouring state of Washington) until 1830, when the native tribes were decimated by malaria – a scourge that raged across the whole American continent for the whole of the nineteenth century. A canal and a lock were built in 1896, allowing safer navigation. Finally, in 1938, the construction of the Bonneville Dam meant that the Columbia River's rapids were submerged.

San Francisco, rough seas near the Golden Gate

'The month of September in San Francisco is the strangest of all. Day and night, the fog comes in through the Golden Gate and spreads over the bay, invading the streets of the city. It gets in everywhere, enveloping people and things, veiling the streetlamps. The occasional passer-by emerges from an ocean of fog . . . and men appear and vanish like ghosts. . . . There is neither day nor night, neither sun nor moon nor stars, just this fog in which a voice can be heard, like a sung lament of the dead, of souls lost by drowning, the powerful sound of the San Francisco foghorn' (Edouard Lavergne, 1941). San Francisco has always been a city of fog, and this climatic phenomenon, particularly frequent during the summer, makes such a strong impression that it often seems nine out of ten visitors will start their description of the city by mentioning the fog.

San Francisco, Cliff House

The famous Cliff House is today a protected site and forms part of the Golden Gate National Recreation Area. The original building was erected in 1863 by the architects Butler and Buckley. An unpretentious structure, it was nonetheless frequented by the big San Francisco families (Hearst, Stanford, Crocker) and by three presidents of the United States, who signed in the visitors' book. It burned down in 1894 and was replaced by an imposing creation (seen here) in the 'French château' style, at a cost of $50,000, by Adolf Sutro, a multi-millionaire and future mayor of San Francisco. Cliff House was not a hotel, but for those who had the money it offered reception rooms, private apartments, and a panoramic dining room with a view over the sea and Seal Rock. It also housed a large art gallery and a permanent exhibition of mineralogy. Cliff House survived the earthquake of 1906 but was destroyed the following year in another fire. Adolf Sutro's daughter, Emma, took over, financing the construction of the third Cliff House in 1909, a Neoclassical building. This is the structure that exists today, which was acquired by the National Parks in 1977.

California, the mission of San Juan Capistrano

The Spanish missions of California do not date back to the beginning of Spanish colonization (1542) but to the end of the eighteenth century. It was Franciscan brothers who came to settle here on the Californian coast; they undertook the task of converting the Indians, putting them in the service of God and the land. The mission of San Juan Capistrano, founded in 1776, was characteristic of the so-called mission style, but its great church was destroyed by earthquake in 1812, burying some forty worshippers in the rubble. The missions were secularized in 1833, and many fell into disrepair.

Yosemite, the 'Three Graces' at Mariposa Grove

In the Yosemite Valley, at Mariposa Grove (literally the 'grove of butterflies'), the gigantic trunks of the giant sequoias soar into the sky. A horse-drawn carriage, tiny by comparison, follows the forest path, passing the group of trees known as the 'Three Graces'. In this part of the forest there are over two hundred sequoias, some standing more than 80 metres (260 feet) high, whose trunks measure 30 metres (100 feet) in diameter and whose bark is 30–60 centimetres (12–24 inches) thick. However, despite their invincible appearance, the sequoias are vulnerable: their roots do not penetrate very deep. When Galen Clark visited this place in 1857, he discovered one of these giants, the 'Fallen Monarch', lying on the ground but still living. The giant sequoias can live for one thousand, two thousand, three thousand years: the oldest trees in Yosemite were there one thousand years before Christ was born.

Los Angeles, a Chinese pharmacy

You might almost think you were in a Taoist temple, but this is a Chinese apothecary's shop in Chinatown, Los Angeles. Unlike in San Francisco, the Chinese of Los Angeles do not live in the same area; they are spread across the whole city, and Chinatown is today where they often have their businesses. The French journalist Jules Huret wrote of a similar shop, with its 'multicoloured façades, curved roofs, with gilding . . . greenish animal entrails . . . dried vegetables, apothecary's displays of burnt herbs, beyond which the pharmacists can be seen, with an everlasting smile on their lips, hacking licorice sticks into tiny pieces, or rolling pills between the tips of their long nailed fingers'.

California, on the circular bridge of the Mount Lowe Incline Railway

An engineer and inspired inventor, Thaddeus Sobieski Constantine Lowe left New Hampshire in 1888 and retired to Pasadena, California. There he and David Macpherson – a railway engineer – and invested in the construction of a railway line intended to run from Pasadena to the top of Mount Wilson. The passengers who are squeezed into this carriage, looking straight ahead of them, must have placed a great deal of faith in the railway's engineering as it curved round the rock face, offering vertiginous views of Los Angeles below. The Mount Lowe Railway eventually brought about its founder's ruin. The elements and various outbreaks of fire got the better of the installations, and the circular bridge shown here was destroyed by torrential rain in 1938. Mr Lowe's railway in the clouds disappeared for ever.

Milwaukee, Wisconsin Avenue

In nineteenth-century Milwaukee the German
community represented three quarters of the
population, and the town came to be called 'New
Frankfurt'. An important port on the western shore
of Lake Michigan, Milwaukee for a long time lived
by its trade in furs and wood. It is also the capital
of beer-making: the biggest breweries in the United
States are based here, and one of them has as its
slogan: 'The beer that made Milwaukee famous!'
This splendid building, which was finished in
1891, was the headquarters of the Pabst Brewing
Company; built in a northern Renaissance style,
it would not look out of place on the banks of the
river Main.

Lake Michigan, the Soo Locks, Sault Sainte-Marie

The only passage from Lake Superior to the other
Great Lakes, the St Mary's River was once hard to
navigate because of the rapids that occurred at
regular intervals along its length (the Ojibwa Indians
travelled on it by canoe, as did the white newcomers
who arrived in the seventeenth century). The first
canal was built in 1797, and in 1855 two large locks
were constructed at Sault Sainte-Marie, the so-called
Soo Locks, close by the Canadian border. In 1881
traffic reached such a volume that the locks were
placed under the management of the US Army's
Corps of Engineers. The strange cigar-shaped ship
pictured here is a 'whaleback', a flat-bottomed cargo
vessel with a rounded superstructure, conceived
by Captain Alexander McDougall in 1886–87 and
especially designed to sail on the Great Lakes.

The grain elevators of the Chicago River

On a visit to Chicago in 1900, one European
traveller was shocked by the heavily industrialized
banks of the Chicago River: 'Some districts . . . appear
to be avenues through hell; streets are divided by
metal bridges thrown up in building sites and factory
yards; twenty, thirty, sixty railway lines, where trains
run unceasingly ... carving up the ground beneath
you. You can see no more than 30 metres [100 feet]
ahead of you. Opaque clouds of steam like fog boils
up above monumental chimneystacks.' In the docks,
'forty grain elevators, these immense reservoirs
that clutter the quaysides of the river, deal with
3 thousand million litres [800 million gallons] of
grain per year'.

Boston, Old State House

Of the Old State House, built in 1713, only the
walls faced with brick survived the fire of 1747.
The building was reconstructed in 1798, and used
for many different purposes, both municipal then
commercial, and suffered as a result; in 1905 the
ground floor was even used as a metro station.
In 1907 Joseph Everett Chandler – an architect
from the Massachusetts Institute of Technology
specializing in heritage preservation – was given
the task of restoring the building to its original state.

New York, the Flatiron Building

The Flatiron Building stands twenty-four storeys high, its strange silhouette dominating the crossroads of Broadway and Fifth Avenue where it joins 23rd Street. On account of its unusual aerodynamic profile, winds blow around the base of the Flatiron. In the early decades of the twentieth century these air currents would lift the edges of women's skirts, revealing their ankles, and curious types would stand around on the corner of 23rd Street to catch the show. This purportedly gave rise to the expression '23 skidoo', used to warn of the arrival of the New York police, who would firmly send voyeurs on their way.

New York, South Street Quay and the Brooklyn Bridge

This dock was where many travellers, famous and lesser known, first touched American soil in the age before steam power. It is marvellously evoked in Walt Whitman's famous poem 'Crossing Brooklyn Ferry' (1900):

'I too many and many a time cross'd the river,
    the sun half an hour high . . .
Look'd toward the lower bay to notice the arriving
    ships,
Saw their approach, saw aboard those that were
    near me,
Saw the white sails of schooners and sloops – saw
    the ships at anchor,
The sailors at work in the rigging, or out astride
    the spars . . .
The large and small steamers in motion, the pilots
    in their pilot-houses . . . '

Atlantic City, a sand-sculptor

'Don't forget the worker!' states this sand sculpture
on the beach at Atlantic City. The gentleman-artist is
putting the finishing touches to his masterpiece and
awaiting visits – and generous contributions – from
morning bathers. In a few hours the beach will look
like the picture on the opposite page, invaded by
holidaymakers in Belle Epoque clothing: striped
bathing costumes and knee-length shorts for the
men, and calf-length dresses and sailors' collars for
the women.

On the beach at Atlantic City

The coast of New Jersey benefits from a sunny climate and the effects of the Gulf Stream, which warms the Atlantic waters enough to allow bathing. Absecon Island, the barrier island where Atlantic City grew up, was once the summer destination of the Lenni-Lenape Native Americans, who came here to fish. In 1670 the first white man set foot on Absecon Island; his name was Thomas Budd, an Englishman, and he was followed in 1754 by Jeremiah Leeds, who came from a neighbouring village. Jeremiah and his family were the first official residents of the island, and in 1839 Millicent Leeds, Jeremiah's second wife, opened a tavern (Aunt Millie's Boarding House) on the site of today's Baltic and Massachusetts Avenues. From this date the city developed rapidly, and in 1854 the first train arrived on the Camden–Atlantic City Railroad, financed by Jonathan Pitney and constructed by Richard Osborne, who gave the new station its name: Atlantic City. As for Pitney, he had the idea to name the streets running parallel to the sea after the great seas and oceans of the world (Pacific Avenue, Baltic Avenue, Mediterranean Avenue, etc.), while the others bore the names of American states. Fifty years later, the Atlantic City Boardwalk was the place to be seen, and the big hotels were never empty. In 1976 gambling was legalized and casinos began to appear, which brought in a great deal of income for the city.

Pennsylvania, Riverside Drive

The state of Pennsylvania owes its name to William Penn, a Quaker who obtained a portion of American territory between Lake Erie and the Atlantic Ocean by Royal Charter from Charles II of England. So, at the beginning of the seventeenth century, Philadelphia, the 'city of brotherly love', and Pennsylvania (literally 'Penn's Woods') were born. At the centre of Pennsylvania, in the Appalachian Mountains, the Allegheny Plateau is a magnificent region covered with luxuriant forests and watered by the Susquehanna River. Long before the arrival of the Europeans, the Iroquois lived on the banks of the river, but in the seventeenth century they gave up their place to the Lenape people. It was with this tribe that Penn negotiated the right to settle a colony in the Alleghenies in 1772. Penn was guided by his 'inner light': he was a pacifist, and welcomed all those who were persecuted or badly treated in neighbouring states. This generosity and tolerance are at the root of the anachronisms that we associate with Pennsylvania – the Mennonite community, for example, who are hostile to 'progress' and who continue – like the Mormons – to travel by horse and cart.

Charleston, the gardeners of the Magnolia Plantation and Gardens

As a southern state, South Carolina and its capital, Charleston, fiercely resisted the forces of the Union, from which they withdrew in 1860, thus sparking off the Civil War. In 1865, having suffered bombardments and a blockade that had lasted for four years, starving the population, Charleston capitulated. The city's architecture is markedly 'Southern colonial', with its villas and gardens in a tropical but rather 'English' style. South Carolina's subtropical vegetation is a wonder: the Frenchman Edouard Lavergne, who knew the area between the two world wars, wrote that 'Charleston is an oasis in North America. The spring in South Carolina, with its azaleas, the wisteria in flower and the laughter of the old black gardeners . . .'. He recalled how in his childhood he would visit the Magnolia Gardens every spring, 'to see the azaleas flowering beside the Ashley River'. This image of the Magnolia Gardens and its staff dates to about 1900.

Mississippi, inside a cotton factory

At the end of the nineteenth century, the region of cotton plantations – known as the 'Cotton Belt' – stretched from the Gulf of Mexico to the Atlantic coast, encompassing the south of Kentucky, part of Tennessee, Missouri and Oklahoma, the east of Arkansas and Texas, the north of Florida, and of course the states of Mississippi, Louisiana, Alabama, Georgia, North and South Carolina and Virginia – almost a quarter of the whole Union in total. In Mississippi, the European slave traders, who had been engaged in the slave trade since the seventeenth century, provided planters with over 30,000 slaves for the period 1783–93 alone. The invention of the 'cotton gin' machine in 1793 had the effect of increasing this traffic even more, which continued until the Civil War. Tennessee Williams, a native of Columbus, Mississippi, evoked the

atmosphere of a cotton plantation in the 1930s: 'It was the end of the afternoon. The cotton gins, fitted with their pneumatic pipes, were still at work pumping up the harvest. A fine cotton dust floated in the sunny air, from the other side of the old road and across the fields.'

New Orleans, St Charles Avenue

In New Orleans, French and Spanish colonial
influences have left a mark on the urban landscape
and the city's way of life. St Charles Avenue, seen
here, displays solid buildings with square towers
in the Spanish style, cast-iron balconies, coloured
façades and loose paving stones – all of which are
reminiscent of cities on the Mediterranean. The
population of New Orleans is racially very mixed –
a combination of Creoles, African Americans, and
of course the Cajuns, ancestors of the French who
were chased out of Canada in 1755 and who found
refuge in the *bayous* (swamps) of the Mississippi
Delta. New Orleans has long been considered the
birthplace of jazz, which evolved as black music
in the city's cellars at exactly the time this picture
was taken. The French Quarter still rings with the
sounds of jazz and Cajun blues.

Florida, St Augustine, Charlotte Street

Florida is a flat peninsula 700 kilometres (435 miles) long that extends into the Atlantic Ocean, enclosing the Gulf of Mexico. It is a 'tourist paradise' of white sandy beaches and little islands; its tip submerges itself in the swamps of the Everglades and reaches still further south into the coral archipelago of the Florida Keys. Discovered in 1513 by the Spaniard Juan Ponce de León, who landed near St Augustine, Florida has a long and tortured history. The Spanish, French and English fought over it, and all fought against the Seminole people, who were chased back to their original territory after three wars between 1820 and 1855. St Augustine, the first colonial town in Florida, is also the oldest town founded by Europeans in the United States. The architecture of the houses lining Charlotte Street displays the vernacular style adopted by the 'Crackers', settlers who came Florida in the nineteenth century: brick chimneys, steep roofs tiled with cypress wood, and timbered gables. In the later nineteenth century St Augustine expanded rapidly: Henry Flagler, a railway magnate and hotel investor, is said to have invested more than 40 million dollars in the development of Florida. The opening of the Hotel Ponce de Leon in 1884 marks the beginning of the town's role as a tourist destination.

Florida, on the Ocklawaha River

The Ocklawaha River flows through the north-east of Florida and today is enclosed by the Ocala National Forest. Sometimes calm and muddy, sometimes swift, it runs through a region of lakes, ponds covered with water lilies, and dense forests, where cypress and a particular variety of maple tree thrive. One hundred species of fish, two hundred species of birds and three hundred species are protected within the park: since the nineteenth century this exceptional environment has been threatened by high levels of pollution, initially from the high volume of steamers navigating the river. During the first half of the nineteenth century the Ocklawaha River was used to transport troops to fight against the Seminole; and in times of peace the river carried tourist steamers like the one shown here. There is still river traffic on the Ocklawaha River today, but the Ocala National Forest is being closely monitored from an ecological standpoint.

372 Bahamas

Bahamas

Nassau, East Street

The capital of the former Lucayan Islands (named after the South American Indians who lived there), Nassau has a rich ethnic and cultural history. The Spanish, the English (it was a Crown colony from 1718), West Africans, pirates and emigrants from South America have all given this town its unique character. Its population grew at the end of the eighteenth century and especially during the nineteenth, thanks to American Loyalists opposed to the Union who arrived here with their slaves, and, later, freed slaves looking for work and a new life. Photographed in about 1900, when Nassau still belonged to the British Crown, this street belongs to a peaceful colonial city, with its colonnaded villas shaded from the burning sun by the closed blinds on the verandas. The light glares on the road and the sky is white with heat. The Bahamas today are synonymous with holidays and 'beach paradise', and with Blackbeard and Calico Jack Rackham, famous pirates of heroic times past. The Bahamas gained full independence in 1973 but still belong to the Commonwealth.

Cuba

Havana Cathedral

South-west of the Bahamas is Cuba, the largest of the Greater
Antilles. Havana, which looks out over the Straits of Florida,
was founded in 1519 by the Spanish. The city grew substantially
during the course of the seventeenth century thanks to its busy
port: gold, silver and gems pillaged by the conquistadors in
Mexico and Peru came this way. Around the time it was seized
by the British, in 1762, a large part of this traffic consisted of
thousands of black slaves headed for the sugar-cane plantations.
This brief intervention by the English ended with Cuba being
restored to Spain in exchange for Florida. The Spanish
constructed a formidable fortress known as San Carlos de la
Cabaña, and in 1789 the grand cathedral of San Cristobal; a jewel
of Hispanic Baroque architecture, it was referred to by the Cuban
writer Alejo Carpentier as 'music set in stone'. This photograph
shows the cathedral square in the last decade of the nineteenth
century, shortly before the 'liberation' of Cuba by the Americans.

Havana, Teatro Tacón

During the course of the first half of the nineteenth century, the wealthy colonists of Havana led a luxurious and socially busy life while the Creoles and black population continued to suffer from repression. This culminated in the uprising of 1868, which turned into a war against the United States that Cuba lost. The city, made up of 80 per cent white and Spanish inhabitants, was called the 'Paris of the Antilles' on account of its sumptuous houses and prestigious official buildings. The Teatro Tacón opened in 1838 to a brilliant season of opera. Ballets and concerts were also given, in which some of the greatest artistes of the time performed (Pavlova herself once made an appearance). Modifications designed to enlarge the building were unsatisfactory, and it was finally pulled down in about 1908 and replaced with a new theatre in the German neo-Baroque style, which opened in 1915. This photograph of the original building dates from between 1890 and 1900. The new Teatro Tacón became the home of the National Ballet of Cuba in 1950, and since 1985 has been known as the Grand Theatre of Havana.

Street in Old Havana

This is how a typical Havana street looked at the turn of the twentieth century in the district known today as 'Old Havana', the historic centre of Cuba's largest city. Straight, narrow and neatly paved, this street would have been laid out by Spanish urban planners in the eighteenth century. Its shops and houses are the classic colonial style, with their façades painted in warm colours and their iron balconies. A strange mood pervades this picture: the men on the street corner and the hairdresser waiting for customers watch the photographer with some suspicion, and the scene seems lacking in characteristic Cuban joie de vivre. It is tempting to read into this atmosphere signs of the deep political and social unrest that would soon make themselves felt.

The invention of the photochrome

The discovery of photography was an enormously important development for the nineteenth century, and among its many early techniques and manifestations was the 'Photochrom' process. The trade name 'Photochrom' of course derives from 'photography' ('writing with light') and from 'chrom', meaning 'colour', and would therefore appear to mean simply 'photography in colour'. But it is not quite as simple as it first appears. In the nineteenth century the difficulty lay not so much in inventing something as in finding an appropriate name for the invention. And since competition was fierce, the great number of inventions combined the relatively small number of Greek and Latin roots meant that the neologisms used to christen some of these were sometimes less than clearcut.

Contrary to what its name suggests, the Photochrom process did not consist of shooting a picture in colour in the way that we would today when we use traditional film: it is rather a process of making colour images out of a single shot that was originally taken in black and white. It must therefore not be confused with 'photochromic' processes, which is a generic terms used to define the process of shooting pictures in colour.

The Photochrom process was devised by the Swiss firm of Orell Füssli and Co., whose head office is in the German-speaking canton of Zurich (which explains the absence of the final 'e' in Photochrom). It was the subject of a patent submitted in Switzerland, France, the United States and, one may presume, in other European countries such as Germany, Italy and Great Britain.

The French patent was registered on 4 January 1888 for Orell Füssli and Co. by the Bletry brothers, 2 Boulevard de Strasbourg, Paris. It was published on 20 March of the same year with the number 187971. Here is the complete text for the patent:

Descriptive memorandum registered in support of the patent of invention by Messrs Orellfüssli [sic] & Co. in Zurich for: process permitting the photographic transference of the original onto litho or chromographic printing plates, with the aid of a single negative.

Despite all progress in the arts of reproduction, it has been impossible until now to prepare, with the aid of photography and *by means of a single negative proof,* an optional number of colour printing plates.

We have succeeded in attaining this goal and this is our method.

On stones or metallic plates & whether the surface is grainy or smooth, a layer of asphalt is poured that is sensitive either to daylight or electric light.

Once the exposure is completed as required, one may proceed with developing, an operation that consists of bringing out the subject again on the plate using turpentine or another soluble substance.

This developing process is then followed, as required, by another that consists of treating the subject with a liquid coating and by a solution, either strong or weak, this last operation being indispensable for obtaining the desired effect.

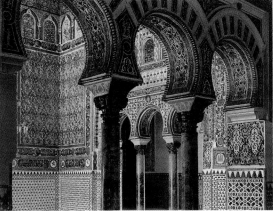

(far left) A retoucher at work in the studio of the Detroit Photographic Company. Photograph by T. S. Bruce and A. Braithwaite (1913)

(left) Hall of the Ambassadors, Alcázar, Seville (Photochrom Zürich, *c.* 1890)

In summary we hereby enter our claim:

The process consisting of directly transferring originals of every kind (and therefore including half-tones) by means of a single negative onto lithographic stones or onto metallic plates whose surface may be either smooth or grainy and made sensitive to light; and to fix and develop these images onto stone or onto metallic plates with the print of the original image (in case of colour printing a number of plates of whatever kind desired from a single negative).

Paris, 4 January 1888
With the authorization of the firm of Orellfüssli and Co.
[signature]

The authors of this patent have clearly kept it all rather vague. It is the general rule of patents: never set out anything in detail, or present intentionally false information in order to keep competitors in the dark. However, this patent does give us a few facts, and looking at the images themselves fills in the gaps. The Photochrom process is not purely photographic but combines lithographic printing with photography. In fact, the technique of transferring photographic images onto stone was already well known. The French lithographer Rose-Joseph Lemercier had registered a patent in 1852 for a technique that he called 'lithophotography', using Judean bitumen (asphalt) as a photosensitive

substance; and some time later, in 1855, the French chemist Alphonse Poitevin registered a similar process that he called 'photolithography', which used albumen or bichromated gelatin.

The real distinction of the Photochrom process lies not in its transference to a lithographic stone, but in its chromatic possibilities. It is, of course, on that point that the patent is silent and about which we must draw our own conclusions. It is not a very difficult to do so. The only way to obtain a colour image from a black-and-white negative is to recreate the colours artificially, 'selecting' each by hand from the monochrome image. Each selection is printed in the chosen colour, and successive layers of overprinting (between four and twenty in total) in different-coloured inks create a colour image.

One way in which this was achieved was to work from the original negative, copying and retouching by hand to produce a partial negative for each colour, which would then be transferred onto a separate stone. The second method consisted of copying the original negative on to as many stones as necessary and then modifying the stones themselves so that only part of the image corresponding to a particular colour would print. This second solution was technically more difficult but it was possible. These are the two techniques that must have been used, perhaps in combination. Whatever method the studios* chose, outstanding professionals were required for every step of the process: photographers to take the original negatives, colour retouchers and laboratory

---

* Photoglob Zurich – the company created by Füssli to distribute his invention – was not the only firm to produce Photochrom images. Other studios had obtained a licence from the firm to use the technique. These included: Keitz & Meiners in Berlin, Raphael Tuck & Sons in London, Photochrom Company Ltd in London, and the Detroit Photographic Co. in Detroit.

technicians to manually selection the colours and
transfer images onto the stones, and designers and
lithographic printers to produce the final image.

Careful observation of the photochromes
allows us to draw several conclusions. For instance,
one original negative could be turned into several
different versions. Differences in coloration
between two photochromes based on the same
image proves either that the same combination
of stones was used but with a change of ink tones
between one and the other, or that we are dealing
with two different sets of colour components
(that is, two different combinations of stones).
The subtle gradations of tone that were sometimes
achieved, particularly in the skies, were achieved
on a single stone by the skilful use the roller, which
was loaded with two different tones of the same
colour, dark above and light below. Examining two
proofs of the same photochrome can in some cases
throw up more important variations: the addition
or suppression of people or other elements, which
reveal that a subtle process of correction, masking
and retouching had taken place on an intermediate
negative before it was copied onto the stone.
The addition of new elements of course implies the
use of a second negative. It therefore seems likely
that the publishers collected 'libraries' of usable
fragments – people, landscapes, etc. – on which
they could draw as necessary in order to 'improve'
the appearance or 'credibility' of the scenes in front
of them. The slow decline of lithography after the
First World War did not necessarily mean the
disappearance of the Photochrom process. Offset
lithography began to replace traditional lithography
little by little, but the Photochrom process adapted
to the new printing technique quite naturally. In
Chicago, the German-born publisher Kurt Teich
used it from the 1920s right up until the end of the
1950s to produce a long series of postcards of
American towns. But that is another story.

Christian Laucou

Index

Page numbers refer to captions and related content. Place names mostly reflect those current at the time the photochromes were made, between 1890 and 1914.